The Joy of Giving
is the
Joy of Living

Betty Schoenbaum A Life Remembered

...As told to Gus Mollasis

Sarasota, Florida

Copyright © Betty Schoenbaum, 2018

All rights reserved. Published by the Peppertree Press, LLC. The Peppertree Press and associated logos are trademarks of the Peppertree Press, LLC.

No part of this publication may be reproduced, stored in a retrieval system, transmitted in any form or by any means, electronic, mechanical, photocopying, recording, or otherwise, without prior written permission of the publisher and author/illustrator.
Graphic design by Rebecca Barbier.

For information regarding permission,
call 941-922-2662 or contact us at our website:
www.peppertreepublishing.com or write to:
the Peppertree Press, LLC.
Attention: Publisher
1269 First Street, Suite 7
Sarasota, Florida 34236

ISBN: 978-1-61493-559-9

Library of Congress Number: 2018900415

Printed May 2018

A Foreword by Gus Mollasis

She's been around our planet for over 100 years. And because of that simple fact, the world is a better place. Raised during the depression, her mindset and attitude hardly ever sink to those blue notes that most of us succumb. It is this attitude that is both her edge and her greatest weapon as she battles to make the world—hers, yours and mine—a much more meaningful and compassionate place. It is this attitude, which is both contagious and rewarding, that will disarm even the most cynical amongst us to let down our guard as we open up our heart a little bit more. But why? The answer is clear and without doubt to this woman named Betty Schoenbaum. To her, our greatest duty is to give—give—of ourselves, to others, for the good of others. If that's her philosophy, then this is her slogan and words that she lives by: "The Joy of Giving is the Joy of Living." Give. It's a beautiful four letter word that when placed at the helm of this lady, who in pounds, weighs no more than her gifted age of 100, takes on new meaning, weight, and power. Once touched by her, especially if it's in the form of hug, you will never be the same, and you will no doubt feel better. There is something special and spiritual about this woman from Dayton, Ohio, who nabbed the Big Man on Campus, an All-American football player from Ohio State, her real life Big Boy beau, who was on his way to creating one of the biggest restaurant chains in American history—Shoney's. Like a great mate, she always stood by her man, and heck, she even helped her Alex name the chain.

When you are with Betty Schoenbaum, you feel that all things are possible and you notice the little things a little more—even if it's from her breathtaking penthouse view that looks at the beautiful Sarasota bayfront. As you look out the windows with Betty, you can't help but be taken in by her view and vison of the world and all things big and small. You feel like you can see and smell a blade of grass on the ground that's hundreds of yards below. While with her, you have the ability to dream, big cloud-like dreams, yet be grounded by the reality of the real world that we all live in.

In Betty's world, her life is built between two important pillars, one being a giving and gracious heart and nature that willingly gives to the world. The second, and the most important part of her legacy, is her family. She will be the first to tell you as she looks proudly at a photo of a family gathering, filled with sons, daughters, son- and daughters-in law, grandchildren, great-grandchildren, and anyone else lucky enough to be in her clan.

None of this would have happened if she hadn't married Alex Schoenbaum. No, none of that would have been possible. And what a loss that would have been. Not only to her large, loving, and beautiful family. But what a loss it would have been had she not graced the planet with her grace and her ability to do the thing that she does best, and that's give.

She will tell you how lucky and blessed she has been in her life. When she says it, you believe every word because you feel it in your heart—heart to heart. It is something she lives by. A little hug is a gift that she gives anyone blessed enough to be in her presence. That little hug—one more example of her giving.

And giving is something that Betty does. Always has and always will. As a small child, she learned the great lesson of giving from her poor grandma as she placed spare coins in a tin box to buy land in Israel. As an adult, she watched her husband raise and give away millions to worthy causes close to his heart. Then after her Alex passed away, she took the torch that was given to her by her beau and kept him alive by giving to his causes, while finding some of her own causes to support. As she continues to forge her own pathway of giving, she has simple criteria in order for her to give. If it helps people go further in education, treasure the arts, value their environment, and is just good for the planet and she is passionate about it, then she will do what comes naturally to her. She will give. And because she does, the world is a better place, because she herself is a gift to our world that, thank God, just keeps giving.

If there is one caveat or lesson to her giving, and something that she has willingly shared with fellow philanthropists, it is this: "Why wait until you are gone to give away what you have been fortunate to earn? Give while you are living, so that you see all the good that your giving does while you are alive." It's this philosophy that has helped build an educational complex and center that benefits Ethiopian Jews in Israel. Think about that a minute. It's this philosophy that's helped thousands of students with scholarships to earn degrees and pursue their life's goals and dreams.

Her giving knows no bounds and can be felt and seen in three places that she has called home in her blessed life: her revered birthplace of Dayton, Ohio; her adopted home of Charleston, West Virginia for 72 years; and her final beloved home on this planet, Sarasota, Florida. All three places she's called home and all have benefited immeasurably by her large and giving heart. Her fourth home, in essence, a home to all the Jews of the world, Israel, has felt her presence and generous spirit in ways best measured, perhaps in biblical and soulful terms, that connect her to a heritage, and traditions best understood by God.

Betty Schoenbaum—she comes from another time and place—a simpler time. A time of a little more innocence. A time when a handshake meant something. A time when families sat down at the table and talked to each other—actually talked to each other without a text, a tweet, or a smart phone interrupting the flow of conversation. A time of summer cottages and fishing on the dock. A time when marching bands greeted a new business that came to town. A time when boys and girls went steady. A time of necking. A time of hot dogs and watermelon on the fourth of July. A time not only to dream the American dream, but a time when you worked hard together to accomplish it. A time when we were grateful for all the good times. And finally, a time to take the time to give something back to those not so lucky and not so blessed, because it was not only the right thing to do, but also because it felt so darn good. This is the time that Betty Schoenbaum comes from. As she's taken the paddle boat down the river in her life, she has always had time to sit and listen to someone and see if she could help make their world a little bit better. In doing so she has made all of our worlds a little bit better. Somewhere in another time and place, I can see an old All-American football player looking down and saying, "Betty, you done Good."

When I asked her what her life has been like—what it felt like to spend time with her beloved family; or give a scholarship away to someone and have it really change their life; or provide the underprivileged with food or shelter, while giving them a little hope. She looked at me with that one-in-a-million saintly smile, and uttered, "Ineffable Joy. That is Joy that's beyond description."

I know what you mean Betty—it's the same feeling I get every chance I've gotten to sit down with you.

Ineffable Joy, indeed.

Thank you for giving me a chance to tell your story.

In gratitude and with one giant hug,
heart to heart,

—Gus Mollasis

Table of Contents

PART ONE
Beginnings – Our Years in Ohio

CHAPTER 1 - My Family Roots	3
CHAPTER 2 - Mother and Daddy	9
CHAPTER 3 - Growing Up & Dating in Dayton	15
CHAPTER 4 - Summers at the Cottage	18
CHAPTER 5 - A Dancer's Life	23
CHAPTER 6 - Getting an Education, Ohio State, & Meeting Alex	28
CHAPTER 7 - Making a Buck, from Autos to Insurance	39

PART TWO
Making Our West Virginia Home

CHAPTER 8 - Huntington & Charleston, West Virginia	49
CHAPTER 9 - Shoney's	53
CHAPTER 10 - Married to an Entrepreneur	63
CHAPTER 11 - Mother's Day with All My Children	67
CHAPTER 12 - Blessings & Shock: A Baby at 48	83
CHAPTER 13 - Synagogue Life & Traditions	92
CHAPTER 14 - Charity Begins at Home	102

PART THREE
Settling Down in the Sunshine State

CHAPTER 15 - On the Move: Florida	117
CHAPTER 16 - World Traveler	123
CHAPTER 17 - Empty Nest	127
CHAPTER 18 - Losing Her All-American	142

Photo Gallery — 158

PART FOUR
Betty's New Life without Her Big Boy

CHAPTER 19 - Philanthropy Takes Center Stage — 177
CHAPTER 20 - Hugs — 189
CHAPTER 21 - My Piano/Art & Artifacts — 192
CHAPTER 22 - A Good Party, Mahjong, & Bridge — 196
CHAPTER 23 - Health and Growing Old — 201

PART FIVE
Reflections on Things That Matter

CHAPTER 24 - Israel — 211
CHAPTER 25 - Grandma Goldman — 226
CHAPTER 26 - Joy of Giving/Joy of Living — 230
CHAPTER 27 - Charleston, West Virginia — 242
CHAPTER 28 - A Lifetime of Blessings — 250
CHAPTER 29 - World Views & the Meaning of Life — 257
CHAPTER 30 - My Family Tree & Me — 268
CHAPTER 31 - Ineffable Joy — 276
CHAPTER 32 - Happy 100th Birthday to Our Beautiful Betty! — 279
Afterword — 283
Appendix — 290

"What I would like to cover"

A preface by Betty Schoenbaum

The first part of my life story, I'll talk about my roots and then from birth to 18 years old. Next, I'll summarize my four years of college, loving marriage, and the advent of my four children. Finally, I'll speak to when I retired from being a mother at 66 and how my life was so astonishing with husband in retirement. However, after he passed away, my life completely changed from a mother to a business woman, handling all his estate matters. My husband had been the giver in the family, but I became the giver, evaluating who I donated to and why I gave to them—why I give is the last part. At the end, I tell everyone that I have been one of the most blessed women in this world and that I could not have lived a more perfect life. There were ups and downs, but the ups were far more beautiful than the downs. And being a Libra, though I'm not a true Libra, the things that have happened in my life and my life story could not be more fantastic. My life has been ineffable. Ineffable means joy beyond description. That's a wonderful word that describes my life. (Tears up)

Part One

BEGINNINGS

OUR YEARS IN OHIO

Chapter 1

My Family Roots

"Everyone has a story. Every story matters."

— Nicole Wedemeyer Miller

When the little girl named Betty Frank was born in the small town of Dayton, Ohio—back in 1917, the world was a much different place than it is today.

That much is easy to see.

What is more difficult to grasp is that child born to Sarah and Sam Frank, her loving parents, almost 100 years ago—is really the same person.

Oh, sure, time has changed her shell.

Her skin and bones are a little brittle.

And the aches for sure are more frequent.

But those eyes—those beautiful eyes that she saw the world with as a little girl—they are still working and connecting her with the ever-changing world.

No, they don't see like they once could. No longer 20-20, but those eyes—those "Betty Schoenbaum eyes"—feel what she sees much better and deeper than they ever did before. The woman who approaches this milestone has seen so much in the last century—the 20th and now well into the 21st century. She has taken in so many changes in this country and in her world. She has witnessed as World Wars raged; prayed as peace treaties were signed; burst with pride as a nation called Israel was born; marveled as men landed on the moon; helped level the equal rights playing field for women; watched as a black man got elected twice to be President of the United States; and suffered the horrors of 9/11 as towers fell and innocents were killed. Between that first day on earth when she arrived, back on September 27, 1917, until the most recent of days, as she approaches September 27, 2017—and her 100th birthday—this little girl named Betty Frank grew into a young lady and filled the role of Mrs. Betty Schoenbaum—forever Alex's girl. In recent years, she's grown into another role that suits her fine—that of the grand lady, who just by her presence graces us all. In between those first days and in the last 100 years, she has fallen in love, married her soulmate, created and nurtured a family tree worthy of celebration, all the while staying focused on her greatest gift and in her life—the thing she sees more clearly than most others—her need to give and her desire to give. It is not lost on the masses, this simple fact that she sees clearly even with failing eyesight.

The ability to give. It is something she encourages in others as she nudges the rest of us with her edict, "Give while you are living to others to the best of your abilities." It is her belief that for this world to remain civilized and survive another hundred years and beyond, we must not only give to each other, but also occasionally give each other a hug.

She didn't know all this stuff back then in the beginning, when she was a little girl—when her name was Frank and not Schoenbaum.

But she knew enough to know the importance of strong roots. What she did know—above everything else—was that she was raised by a family who loved her, and whose roots were planted deep into the soil of her Ohio home and the soul of her being.

Her roots are strong.

This woman named Betty Schoenbaum.

Metaphorically, she is a tree that keeps giving, to all the branches that connect her with her big heart. It is a tree that bears plentiful fruit and will leave a legacy of giving long after she leaves this earth.

Strong roots. Strong convictions. Strong actions.

Strong compassionate results of generous giving.

That is the fruit that is picked from her tree of life.

She may not have known everything about where she came from, but what she did know, was important to her and important to pass down to future generations of her massive family tree—her family roots.

I don't know a lot about my ancestry, because my family didn't talk a lot about them. Our roots are in Europe, but my parents were born in this country. My grandparents and great-grandparents were born in Europe. My fraternal grandparents were born in Lithuania. They changed their name from Olitsky to Joe Frank at Ellis Island.

The Joy of Giving is the Joy of Living

I know on one side of my family, I don't have much of a family tree. My maternal grandmother, Fanny Katzen Goldman, didn't share our history with us. She was the daughter of a rabbi—I do know that. She knew Hebrew, which was unusual, because they never taught a girl Hebrew in the Jewish faith. She was raised in Vilnius, Lithuania.

My grandfather Goldman was killed tragically. He was head man of the horse stables in Poland and then he came to the United States. He and grandmother had already lost twin boys by the time that they arrived here in America.

They came to Ellis Island and he asked where he could get a job training horses. Kentucky apparently was already known for that, which surprised me a bit, because this was in the early 1890s. I don't know how they got there. For all I know, it could have been by a horse and buggy. I don't know—I just know he got to Somerset, Kentucky with his wife and two children.

Once there in Kentucky, he found a job with a man who had a race track, raised animals, and sold the studs.

Then their lives changed drastically.

One Monday morning while grandfather was going to the bank, somebody held him up and took his money. Tragically they shot and killed him.

I believe he was only 32-years-old at the time. This left my grandmother a widow and pregnant with her fourth child. My mother, Sarah, had already been born by this time. So sadly my mother's father was killed and my grandmother was left with what would soon be four children.

Grandma barely knew English. She spoke Hebrew, because

her father who was a rabbi taught her Hebrew. In those days, that was quite unusual. Girls were not taught Hebrew. Boys were taught Hebrew for their bar mitzvahs. Girls were not barmitzvahed or batmitzvahed or confirmed. They were nothing. Girls didn't count—period. The boys were important. My grandmother was very religious and even lived behind the synagogue.

She had a brother in Cincinnati who had a basement and he let her use it for her family. She went to work in cigar box factory. After my grandfather was killed, she married a man who was from Dayton, Ohio, whose last name was Ellman.

But every day, she religiously went over to the synagogue and stood out in the hall, because women were not allowed to be in the same area where the men were praying. Twice a day she prayed. In Hebrew, it's called davening. She davened twice a day in the hall, while the men were in the room religiously twice a day for the rest of her life.

Grandma Goldman. She is the one who taught me to give. She was a beautiful woman. Her name was Fanny Goldman. She had little tin tea boxes. They were called Sweet-Touch Nee tea and the boxes had little gold straps, like trunks. She would cut a slit in the top, and as poor as she was, my grandmother always put money in there every Friday night. It was a nickel or a dime or a penny, but money always went into those three boxes.

I was five years old when I said to her, "Grandma, what do you do with all that money that you put in there?" She said, "I'm saving money to buy land in Palestine (Israel)."

Today the Arabs say that we stole the land. My grandmother

said we were buying the land in Palestine (Israel).

Grandma Goldman was so kind.

I remember once my mother needed a towel for home economics in school, and my grandmother couldn't buy a towel for a nickel, so she took a flour bag and crocheted the end around the side.

My mother was so proud that her towel was the prettiest one in school.

Chapter 2

Mother and Daddy

"Children learn to smile from their parents."

— Shinichi Suzuki

I had the most beautiful parents that any child could have.

The children came first. I don't remember seeing liquor in my home, except in the medicine cabinet. If you got a bad cold, you got hot tea with a little bit of Schnapps in it. That's what they called it, because my father knew German pretty well. His mother was from Germany, so she spoke it and he picked up a few words, but not many.

Mother and Daddy always put us first. To them, we, the children, were everything. I remember my mother schlepping us to dancing classes every day. A YWCA was located next door, so she would go to there while we took our dancing lessons. My brothers worked for my dad in the chicken business even from the time they were 12-years-old.

I called him Daddy. He was handsome—absolutely handsome. In fact, there's a picture of mine, with my sister and my daddy. They look like brothers. My brother, Marvin, was handsome and a tall 6' 2." My brother, Joe, was very social and well-liked.

My father loved cars. I have a picture of me and I'm about a year-and-a-half or two years old sitting on the running board with my sister and my daddy. His foot is on the running board, as if to say, "This is my car and these are my children." The car had whitewalls and Isinglass curtains. There were no windows and it had a top on it. If it was raining you had to get out and put your Isinglass windows up so it wouldn't rain in the car. I don't know what kind of car it was, but for those times, it was an expensive car. Oh, my God, he was so proud of that car. I think he was prouder of that car than he was of his children. He thought cars were wonderful.

Here's an interesting story about my daddy. When he went to get his bicycles fixed at ten years of age, he would go down to Lorraine Avenue to the *Wright Brothers Bicycle Shop*. The Wright Brothers came from Dayton, Ohio.

Daddy was a hard worker, a very hard worker. He would get up at four o'clock in the morning and be down at the chicken plant, the Joe O. Frank Company, named after my grandfather. It's my understanding that it has closed in the last twenty years, but my grandfather started it back in 1888. We had a creamery where we made butter. We asked the farmers to save their eggs for us and we would sell their eggs at market. We would furnish hospitals, hotels, the military, and the Wright-Patterson Air Force Base. We would also furnish all the grocery stores, including a chain called the *Piggly Wiggly* and one called *A&P*. We were the wholesale people and we served everybody poultry, chickens,

Mother and Daddy

turkeys, butter, and eggs.

My father was a change-of-life baby and had six brothers and sisters, who really looked after him. Because their mother really didn't want another baby, he was raised by his brothers and sisters. He was about 13 years younger than his oldest brother.

My mother just adored my father. When he came home from work, she wouldn't let him come in the front door, because he'd been in the plant where they had been killing the chickens. The floors were wet, because they had to be cleaning them all the time. So he had to come around the side of the house and pass by the kitchen window where my mother would hear him whistling. He'd yell to my mother, whose name was Sarah, but my father called her, "Sorky." He'd say, "There's my Sorky."

You could just see the happiness in my mother's eyes.

I just loved the love they had for each other and for us. It was important to see that as a child in all my family. All my brothers and sisters were wonderful people. It made me feel secure as a child. They always put the children first.

We ate dinner at home every night, except for Sunday night. There was a place, a cafeteria called Kuntz's Café. On the way home coming back from the cottage, we'd stop there. Otherwise, we'd go out every Sunday night to Kuntz's. We ate chicken six nights a week and on Friday night, the Sabbath, we always had brisket.

Daddy would go to bed early at night. He'd come home for lunch and take a little nap right over the heat register, because it was always so cold at the plant. It was a big plant with lots of water on the floor. Our truck would go out to the farmers and bring in the eggs and chickens that were in coops. They would go to the creamery and get butter and Saturday morning, they would all go to market. The market was on the inside. They also had stands on the outside, but we were on the inside. We ran it during the week, too, so people could go down there and buy groceries—not wholesale, but fresh stuff—every day and anytime they wanted it. We then opened up stores called, *Tasty-Bird*, all over town. When they closed the market, we opened these stores, and they were open for quite a few years.

When I was a child, we didn't go into the plant very much, but I worked at the plant on Saturdays as a cashier when I was in high school. That was the day you could pick your own chicken out and put your mark on it. We would kill it for you and give you fresh—absolutely fresh—chicken that same day.

Mother and Daddy—they both worked so hard and I don't think we appreciated it, because everybody worked hard back then—even our neighbors did.

Today it's different. In the first place, back then women usually never worked. Or if they did work, they had jobs as a secretary, teacher, or nurse, just the things that women worked at back in the day. It was totally different. Women usually weren't doctors or lawyers or all that.

I wouldn't trade my childhood with anybody in this world. Why? I had the most perfect childhood any child could have. Why would I want more? My parents allowed us to go to Girl Scout Camp and Boy Scout Camp. In fact,

Mother and Daddy

when I was a young mother, I was a den mother and Girl Scout leader after I got married. One of my Girl Scouts lives down here at Sara Bay and she salutes me every time she sees me and says the Scout oath. For about twenty years, I was a Girl Scout cookie chairman, because I had two daughters. My girls did great selling those cookies.

My daddy didn't start the business—his father did and his brothers were in the business, as well. There were six families involved in it. They wouldn't let him do hardly anything. They ran him. They raised him and were used to being his boss. There wasn't anybody who could say anything against my father. He was the sweetest, dearest man. I never heard my father say a curse word. Ever! My mother said a swear word once and he told her about it. That curse word was S * * T.

That's right. In fact, when my daughter came home from camp and said the same word when she was ten years old. I told her, "Go to the mirror and I want you to say that word again. While you're doing that, think that a pile of it is coming out of your mouth." She looked at me and apologized, saying it had just slipped out. Then she told me, "The counselors at camp say it every other word."

The greatest lesson I learned from my parents is this. "If you don't have something nice to say about someone, don't say anything about that person."

Mom and Daddy were very compatible. My mother was a pretty good manager and my daddy needed a little managing, because he was spoiled by his brothers. They were pretty good at finances. When my brothers went into the business, they had so many cousins, they decided to go into other businesses, because they were 15 years younger than the cousins, who were bossing them around.

I remember my mother and daddy as two of the sweetest parents that you could ever have. I knew that I was blessed and lucky to have such beautiful parents whom I loved, respected, and always looked up to.

Chapter 3

Growing Up & Dating in Dayton

"I don't want to date. But I do have dreams about a great love."

— Sophie B. Hawkins

I went to Steele High School in Dayton, Ohio. I was the center on the basketball team, because I was 5' 8½" tall. At that time, back in the 1930s, that was tall. There were other tall girls who didn't have the ability and I was fairly athletic. Right now, not so good. I don't think I could make a shot today. It's been so many years. But back then I was a pretty good shooter and that's why I was a center. I played with my brothers at home, so I knew something about basketball.

I also was on the senior debate team, which was a great honor in that school. I had a teammate and we had to debate against the two smartest boys in the school, Leonard and Philip Stein. The debate subject was whether the United States should own and operate hydroelectric power plants like Canada. It was what was assigned and regarding the subject, it was the most practical side to take when you studied both of them. It constituted part of our senior year class debating requirement. I ended up being one of the better debaters and we ended up winning that debate.

I was very active in school and in theatre. I enjoyed all the skits they performed on the stage. I tap danced in every one of them. I even tap danced with the senior president of the class, who didn't know how to dance at all. My high school was a wonderful experience. I danced in school almost every day. I studied.

I didn't play golf. I always thought golf was a dumb game. Why chase a little ball around the course and get mad at it? Anyway I didn't like it, but I liked and played tennis socially. I played bridge, danced, took music, and played basketball. I was very busy—an all-around American girl.

I had varied interests. My mother wanted me to do everything—play the piano, dance—everything. And I received a lot of training. My mother lived vicariously through her children. She saw to it that all the things she had wanted when she was young, she was able to provide for us.

I was grateful for all the lessons my mother sought out for us. As I've said, I had two of the most beautiful parents in the world. In fact, my brother talked about our father and said, "You know what? Our daddy didn't have a mean bone in his body. He never talked against people. He encouraged people." And maybe that's where I got that from.

My high school days were happy ones, except for one thing—the boys were too short. (Laughs) I wouldn't go with the short boys. Today men like tall women. Men don't mind if a woman towers above them. But back then, men wanted to be the biggest ones, the taller ones, you know.

Growing-up & Dating in Dayton

As far as dating goes, I had one steady boyfriend for three months. He was so aggressive in his driving that I stopped going with him. I just told him, "You're too aggressive when you drive. You have to be first at the light. And I want a laid-back, easy-going person and you are not." That was it.

Dating wisely was rough, because I had a sister who was two years older. She was older, so the boys were taller, but those boys wouldn't date me, because I was my sister's little sister. Well, that's normal. When you're a senior in high school, you don't date a sophomore or freshman. My sister was the most popular girl in the school. Sometimes we had a friendly and unfriendly competition like most sisters. We were on each other's turf. We slept with each other in the same bed. We didn't wear the same clothes, because I was taller and I couldn't wear her hand-me-downs.

Because I was tall, I used to model at the local department store, Rike-Kumler. They asked me to model and on Saturdays quite often I would get $5.00 for modeling. Back then, that's what they paid. We modeled during lunch at the restaurant, where I would go from table to table. During my time at Ohio State, I modeled at Lazarus and received ten dollars. Eventually my rate went up and when I had time during college, I continued to model at Lazarus. It was 1940, in the middle of summer. There was no air conditioning. Yet there I was, modeling fur coats in August with this make-believe igloo on the stage.

Chapter 4

Summers at the Cottage

"The simpler things are, the happier they are."

— Gwyneth Paltrow

I want to talk about my beautiful family and the days at our wonderful cottage on Crystal Lake.

My mother had four children in seven years. Mother would never let us go away to camps like all of our neighbors did. We had to stay home, but my daddy built our family a cottage, so that we could spend every summer there with our grandmother. My parents would go into town and do their work in the daytime and come back and stay with us at night. Then they would go back to work in the morning and my grandmother would watch us.

We lived near a farm, where a man let us milk the cows, ride the tractors, and smell that wonderful new-mown hay. We had a row boat and a canoe on the lake, since no motorboats were allowed. It was a clear spring-fed lake that you could see all the way to the bottom, where you could see the water bubbling up and fish swimming way down there. I grew up and was raised in a veritable heaven. It was paradise.

Summers at the Cottage

Whenever I have an EKG and the nurses tell me to be quiet and relax, I think of Crystal Lake.

Crystal Lake is between Springfield and Dayton, Ohio.

We had the second cottage there with pump water, no plumbing, and no electricity. Dad built it in 1922 for the family as a getaway.

He built that cottage, because mother wanted to belong to the country club. We joined and daddy would be sitting there playing pinochle with some folks he could care less about, while they would listening to Cincinnati Reds baseball games from the radio that was placed in the middle of the table. My father was so bored, because he was a fisherman and he loved to fish. He built this cottage so he could fish and take us out and teach us how to fish. At the cottage, the farmers would lend us their horses to ride.

Our childhood was gorgeous. We had a beautiful home in Dayton as well. It was a five-bedroom three-bath English Tudor, where we lived in the winter. In the summer, we were really just children having the time of our lives.

The cottage had a special name—Four Maples—four maple trees grew in the front yard. It also had a wonderful beach and we built a little diving board. The other people we shared the lake with were named Copenhaver—he was the mayor of Springfield, Ohio. Today that lake is still there, but unfortunately is a subdivision for Wright Patterson Air Force Base. Things have changed. People tell me not to go out there, because I would be horrified at the changes. My brother specifically told me not to go there the last time I visited Ohio.

We built the cottage in 1922 when I was five years old. My

mother had just had her last child and I remember watching him as he rested in her arms. As I recall, the house came from Sears Roebuck. The cottage itself came in a box and was delivered by truck from Sears Roebuck.

We had an outside shower and a one-seater outhouse as the bathroom. The cottage had a screened porch all around two sides and three bedrooms. We had a pump if we wanted water in the kitchen and if we wanted refrigeration, we had an ice box. Our water was hooked up to a spring, so we took cold baths. There were no utility lines installed or water pipes.

It was heaven.

My father kept that cottage up and over the years, he modernized it. We installed electricity, indoor bathrooms, and all other modern conveniences were done later. Our friends and family loved it! All the kids from the country club would come out there for Fourth of July fireworks over the lake.

The Fourth of July at the cottage was so special.

My mother wouldn't know if 100 or 150 or even 200 people might be coming for the fireworks, so she set up flat tables with saw horses. She'd buy lots of watermelons, hot dogs, corn on the cob, and potato salad, so we would have a picnic every Fourth of July. I loved it. And we didn't serve the watermelon on plates—we would just eat it over the grass.

What a life!

We'd drop our lines on the lake every night at the clubhouse. In the morning we couldn't wait to see what we caught. One day we caught a seven-pound turtle, so we had turtle soup that night. I could never bait the hook—Dad had to do it for me. I couldn't put the worm or fish or crawfish on the hook.

We'd catch all kinds of fish. The catfish were marvelous, because the water was so pure and it was the best catfish I ever tasted in my life. We also had trout, little trout, and even a few bass in there. Dad liked to hang out and fish. He loved it and he went fishing with us—my sister Geri and my two brothers, Joe and Marvin.

Marvin is still with us—he is the baby of the family. I was the second-born child—the one who was supposed to be the boy, because the first one is supposed to be. Everyone always wanted a boy first, but my sister came, but that was all right. They loved her and adored her. She was beautiful, as you can see from this picture. She's gorgeous.

And then I came along. I was about seven and a half pounds. But they wanted a boy and here comes another girl. So I am a middle child, and I definitely was treated as a middle child. Then my brother Joe came. And that was God. God had come. That boy had come. And then my mother had Marvin, because she always wanted four children. My sister Geri passed away at 92 and my brother Joe at 90. My brother Marvin is 95 years old, five years younger than me. He lived in Naples, but he lives in Sarasota now. God has blessed us.

I attribute our longevity to eating range-fed chickens growing up. They didn't have hatcheries then. All your chickens had to be range-fed. All my siblings lived in different parts of the country. My sister lived in California, one brother lived in Dayton, Ohio, and my other brother lived in Columbus, Ohio. We lived a very healthy life.

Back at the cottage, we had a raft in the middle of the lake and we'd always hold races to see who could swim out there the fastest. I was never the fastest. My sister was always faster. She always did everything better than me. She did.

Telling these stories today, especially about the cottage, makes me feel like I am there. It was up on a little hill. There were fields all the way around to the right of the cottage. It was like a Norman Rockwell painting. Exactly. I've got a whole book on Rockwell. It takes me back to the good old days. A simpler life. My life was a real simple life. It really was. It sounds exciting with all the dancing and music lessons. I've got a diary. And if you read that diary, I wrote it when I was 15 years old. It was my confirmation year. And in it I say, "I had a date tonight. He's swell." (Laughs) At 14 or 15 I shouldn't use that word. "I went out with a boy tonight. He was so ugly, if he ever asks me out again, I'll never go out with him." (Laughs) I was honest. I was either playing bridge, dancing, going out to the cottage, or going to my music lessons all throughout my diary.

Those were special days—especially those days at the cottage, at Crystal Lake during the summer.

I can still smell the freshly mowed grass.

Chapter 5

A Dancer's Life

*"Dances have a second and third life.
You feel they are never ready. They always have
a chance for another life."*

— Mikhail Baryshnikov

Dancing. I've always loved dancing.

I started my dancing when I was three years old. My sister was five years old and old enough to attend dancing lessons. My mother wanted me to take dance as well. So they had a little toddler's class that I attended when I was three. I remember I had a green dancing dress and my sister wore peach. The room where I took ballet was huge. I had never been in such a big room in my whole life.

I studied in Dayton, Ohio, until I was 18 years old. My sister, Geri, wasn't called Geri back then—she was known as Geraldine. She hated both names, but eventually she settled on answering to Geri. We danced at so many events. I remember my father was the president of the Big Butter, Egg, and Poultry Wholesalers in the state of Ohio. Naturally it was left to me and my sister to perform at every convention that they held. My sister and I would play the piano and violin and we'd tap dance.

And I had this silly song that I played: (SINGING)

> Sometimes I'm happy,
> Sometimes I'm blue,
> Butter and Egg Business depend on you,
> Sometimes the price goes up to the sky,
> But the whole world still loves chicken pie
> Now which came first, the egg or chicken?
> Nobody knows, but they're both good picking
> So get your eggs and chicken too
> That's my advice to you
> You heard me say it, that's my advice to you.

Oh, would we get the applause. We were just kids, but we loved the applause. My mother wanted both of us to be dancers. I took dancing four days a week after school. First we had two years of ballet. I didn't start my tap till I was seven years old. I stopped dancing, because I grew to be too tall. At that time, chorus girls were between 5' 4" and 5' 6". I was 5' 8" by the time I was in high school. This helped me make a big decision. When I got to college, I decided that instead of becoming a dancer, I'd get myself a husband. (Laughs) That's how I got my *M-R-S* in college. That's where I met my husband, Alex. But a lot more on that later.

What dancing did for me was give me one of the greatest things in my life. It gave me confidence. I could get up in front of an audience and speak to them without a note in front of me, and give all my heart to what I was saying. When a person doesn't have to look at a piece of paper and they speak from the heart, the words might not be as proper as they could have been had I written them down, but it came from the heart. And in subsequent years in every one of my speeches, I've been able to influence other people to give, because what I said came from the heart.

Dancing has helped me in so many ways. It gave me poise and confidence. It helped me so that I was not scared to get up a say what I had to say. I was blessed all my life. The ability to dance, especially in my youth when I danced so much, has had healthy benefits that I reap now.

I danced up to the time I was 18. There are many pictures like this one that are part of my scrapbook, including some from the 1920s and 30s at the Bott Dancing Academy.

In all the pictures, the tallest one is always me. Here I am at the end. Looks like a Busby Berkley scene. There are a lot of legs. Good legs too. Dancing legs. I didn't keep in touch with any of those gals, because I moved away from Dayton when I was 22 years old and got married —I never lived in Dayton again. Still, I could tell you a lot of the names of the gals: Winifred Boehm, Charlotte Ryan, Genevieve Schwartzel, Marion Mead, and her sister, Mary. Their parents owned the Mead Corporation. Nancy Patterson is also in there and her father was president of National Cash Register.

At the Bott Dancing Academy, I learned poise and how to get up in front of people and not be afraid. I learned one other thing. I learned that I loved to entertain people and make them laugh and smile. One of the other benefits from dancing was that the exercise made me strong in my bones and everywhere else when I was young.

I love this neat photo of us dancing in lace dresses. It's probably from when we were trying out for the Radio Keith Orpheum (RKO) national talent contest, which we won.

Our dancing class won third place nationally for tap dance. We competed nationally. Here's a picture of us going on a bus to Kansas City RKO National Finals.

It was a very exciting time in my life for a young girl. RKO had a competition and acts from all over the United States competed at all their theatres. In Dayton, we won a contest. In Columbus, Ohio, we won the state contest. The state winners went to Kansas City, where my dancing class won third place nationally. Our award was to be the chorus at the Keith Albee RKO Theater in Brooklyn. When there, we stayed at the St. George Hotel, which had the only swimming pool in New York. This was 1931, and at this time—of course—there was no air conditioning.

I was born on September 27, 1917, so that would have made me 14. I had dreams of dancing and had planned to be a dancer, but I grew too tall. Dancers were shorter back then, but they're all 5'8" to 5'10" today. Now they don't want me anymore, because I'm 5'4" again. Since I turned 95, I've shrunk.

There was no thinking of being a Rockette, because there were no Rockettes at the time. In fact, the chorus at the Roxy Theatre was called the *Roxy-ettes*, which is a forerunner of the Rockettes.

As far as who was the better dancer, my sister was far better than me. She was a Prima Ballerina with the *Ziegfeld Follies* in 1936, when I was a sophomore in college. Then her show went on the road and my parents decided that a nice

Jewish girl does not travel around the country for two- and three-night stands. So they made her come back to Dayton after all those years of dancing. She had regrets. It broke her heart. She was a gifted dancer.

Let me tell you, she did everything so well. Everything she touched, she did well. She was in the National Honor Society when she was a junior, while I had to wait till I was a senior until I got in. She did everything well and of course that gave me a complex. I was a shy child, believe it or not, and very quiet, because she put me down. She loved me, but she thought that she was helping me—instead, she was giving me a complex. I sucked my thumb. And I did that until quite late. In fact, I had to cure myself of that before I went to college, because I was afraid that my roommate would see me sucking my thumb.

Insecurity—I guess that's what it was. But at the time, I didn't realize it, because this was my sister and I was the little sister. I was the one who was never going to get married. Instead, I ended up getting married before she did and I lived a far happier life. She loved me. And I loved her. And I never really felt like it was competition, because I never thought I could compete with her, because she was so talented. And I miss my sister to this day, especially the times we danced together in our youth.

Chapter 6

Getting an Education, Ohio State, & Meeting Alex

"Most of us make up our minds in the first three minutes of meeting someone whether there's a potential for a relationship."

— Helen Fisher

I remember my first day on campus because that was the day I met my husband.

We were both freshman.

Anyway, I felt that I had to go to Ohio State University, because my sister was in New York studying dancing, which was quite expensive at that time. My mother and daddy promised me that when I got to be a junior I could transfer to the Katherine Gibbs Business School in New York after my sister was through with her dancing. That was the deal.

So I met Alex my first year and through our second year we were friends, strictly friends, nothing more. Then eventually we would do a little necking. That was kissing. We called it necking. We always necked, because it wasn't safe to have sex back then. And necking is from the neck up. That's necking.

Getting an Education, Ohio State, & Meeting Alex

From the neck up. (Smiles)

At first we were strictly friends and we didn't do that much necking. He would walk me around the corner, buy me a Coke for a nickel and we'd sit and talk about his career and mine—his football career and my dancing. I danced a lot in college and won a lot of cups for my sorority.

Alex was a very good football player and an All-American in 1938. He beat Michigan two of the three years he played. He didn't play as a freshman. They didn't play freshman until 1973, when the two-platoon football started, an offensive 13-man team and a defensive 13-man team.

Let's talk about how I got to Ohio State.

When I first got to Ohio State, I went into architecture, so for the first two weeks of school they gave us drawing lessons. My art was lousy. Nowadays they have computers to do the pictures. From the time when I was young, I would doodle and draw house plans. I loved to make house plans. My favorite house was the round house which had a balcony around each floor. My design had fireplaces in the rooms and you would go up in the middle of the building. I just loved to sit and doodle, but I couldn't draw. When I saw a straight line, it didn't go obliquely or in different ways. As a test they gave me a bar of Ivory soap to carve the head of a woman. When I handed it in, they gave me an E. An E was failing and I thought what I had carved was gorgeous. So I switched to the School of Business at Ohio State. At that time, not too many women were in the School of Business. As far as architecture, they discouraged me.

So I got into the advertising track. It was becoming very

popular in newspapers and everything. I wanted to be an executive. Women back then were secretaries, teachers, nurses, or maids. They didn't have much opportunity. Those jobs didn't pay much, but being employed by a firm for the kind of work I wanted to do meant I would be paid more. I just felt like I wanted to try for something more than those other things.

I dropped architecture because I couldn't draw and in advertising, I did the business part, not the layout part. For my first quarter I made an A, two B's and an E. The E was in business organization. I was in a one o'clock class and there were 28 jocks in my class. What happened once is they got the final ahead of time and my roommate and I were the only girls in the class and we didn't get the final ahead of time. I got a 91 on the final, because they graded on the curve. The teacher had the final. He thought so much of Alex who was in the class that he let him go over and pick up the finals that were in his office and bring them to the class. They gave all the jocks a test that they could pass so that they could be on the team. My roommate was brilliant and we both got scores above 91 and I'm the only one that failed in the class. The professor, Dr. Bauerly, left Ohio State and became head of the School of Business at Pennsylvania University. Later when we came back for a dinner at Ohio State, I was married to Alex by then. Dr. Bauerly told me that if he knew I had the sense to marry Alex Schoenbaum, he would have given me an A. That's a true story. So I took the class over in the spring. He told me, "I really should give you an A in the class, but you flunked it the first time, so I'm giving you a B." I didn't care. I passed it. Most of the time I got A's and B's, so I did pretty well.

Getting an Education, Ohio State, & Meeting Alex

Like most people, I had to study. I had one teacher who picked me out in the beginning of the class. He talked to me the whole time. I can picture him looking at me right now. When I didn't know an answer, he picked up the eraser and threw it at me. I think he liked me. He was Jewish. I talked to him after class and asked him if he was mad at me. He said, "You're a smart woman and I want you to know everything that I'm teaching you."

I don't think I was smart—I think that I worked hard. I really did. As a matter of fact, my sister said, "You're going to be an old maid because you study too much—you're never going to get a husband." Funny thing is—I got one five years before she did.

I lived in a dorm on campus and worked hard. It's always important to do your best. When you go to school, if you horse around and don't have a schedule, you won't make it that way. You have to study. Still, I like what some schools are doing today, regarding how they teach with innovation. They're calling them schools of innovation. It's where you really have to use your brain. You're not just reading what the books say. You read beyond what the books say and use your brain so you can see how you can improve the program you're studying and open your mind to the subject. Think out of the box. They're doing that now.

I went back my junior year and then in my senior year, Alex asked me to stay out of school, because he was a senior honorary and he was working his way through school. He played football and had a job at Lazarus Department Store when his football team wasn't practicing, so he had very little time to see me.

During my college years I joined the Alpha Epsilon Phi sorority. . I didn't even go to my Dayton University graduation, because I wanted to get my degree from Ohio State—they have a degree for me, but I always wonder where they got it. They said with all that I have done for Ohio State and with the wisdom I have, they felt that I should have a degree from Ohio State behind my name. That's what they have and that's why they put it in. I didn't put it in. It's not an honorary degree, although I have two honorary degrees, one from Ohio State University in business and one from the University of Charleston in humanities.

I spent three years at Ohio State and I finished at Dayton, but I did not get a degree from them. Dayton was a Catholic Boys School, but it's now co-ed and has been for years. I went to night school there, because they did not have school in the daytime for women. Because I was going to Katherine Gibbs, which was a business school, they didn't require that much science. In my undergraduate years at Ohio State, I didn't take much science—I took business courses. So when I went to Dayton University, I didn't have two science hours. I also had to have two physical education courses for each quarter, but I couldn't get them there, because it was a Catholic *Boy's* School. I couldn't have science, because they didn't have the labs open at night. I couldn't get my science, but I took the other subjects I needed. Even though I still could not graduate, the university honored me and that's why I was at the graduation.

That sounds all very confusing, but just know this the first real degree I got was my BS. My Betty Schoenbaum. (Laughs)

But seriously, education is so important in life. You never know what you really have in you, until you're challenged. And an education will challenge your ability. Back in the day, it was important for the boy to have the education. Well, my parents felt that we all should have a college education. Mother wasn't too happy when I didn't want to go, because I was with Alex and he had given me his fraternity pin as a junior.

Back then, Alex and I were doing a little necking—actually we did a lot of hugging and kissing.

I remember meeting him the first day of school. We were both freshman. It seems like it was so long ago. Then this other time, he came down to Dayton with a cousin of mine who lived in Columbus. My cousin was driving down to see me and he said to Alex, "I'm going to Betty Frank's house. Would you like to go?" Alex said, "We've been friends. She's a good friend of mine." So he came to visit us and he walked into my parent's home. We lived in an English Tudor home with leaded glass windows and gables—a lovely home—I think he thought that my family had money. I think he was looking for a rich girl. (Laughs) We weren't rich. We were upper middle class. Thank God. I guess he thought it would be advantageous to go with me. So when we went back to school in the fall for our junior year, he said, "You know what? I think I'm falling in love with you."

I said, "Well, I like you very much. I like your ambition and I admire you." We started going with each other and by Thanksgiving, he had given me his fraternity pin. By spring, he gave me a fraternity ring—a black onyx one. We saw each other on the weekends, if he wasn't busy. He would hitch a ride, thumb his way into Dayton, and then when he was ready to go home, my family would take him out on the highway and he would thumb a ride back to Columbus.

We enjoyed being with each other. My family liked him and everything about him. He passed the family test, but when I told my family that I wanted to marry him, my mother was concerned about his future prospects.

I said, "Mother, Alex made the Honorary Societies of Ohio State." He was a smart guy and he loved business. He really did. But he worked at Lazarus, a big chain department store, after school. In fact, Simon Lazarus was his mentor. In other words, he wanted Alex to stay at Ohio State and he helped out financially.

Alex had his ambitions and how he was going to make his way in life, but the thing is, he never talked about it. He wasn't one of those who spoke about his plans. He had a father who taught him that. And anytime my Alex would go to his father and tell him what he was going to do, his father would always challenge him with, "I bet you can't do it."

Thinking that he would do it to please his father, I told him, "Don't listen to your daddy. You do things to please yourself, not your father. Your father will be gone someday. You do things to please yourself."

I've told my children that same thing. "You don't float on your daddy's coattails—you do it yourself and then you can be proud of yourself and not just of your daddy."

It was very hard for my father-in-law to ever congratulate my husband on his success. That's sad. All four of his children.

Getting an Education, Ohio State, & Meeting Alex

He never really encouraged them, yet amazingly, they are all achievers except for one, the youngest. His brother ran his life. He told him when to jump and when not to jump. So when it came time to split from the family and get married, he didn't know when to jump or not.

When I came out of school, all I wanted to do was get married. Instead of getting a BS I got an MRS. (Laughs) I wasn't smart. I married a boy whose first job was selling dandruff remover, traveling for barber supplies in three states. He found something that took his dandruff out and thought it was the greatest product in the world, so he started selling it. But more on that later.

Back to our beloved Ohio State. It's still a special place to me.

The Ohio State University has always meant a lot to both me and my husband. We have gratefully and proudly done so much for the university. We were on the foundation board for years. When Alex got off the foundation board, I got on at age 79, and was a member until I was 97 years old. I could no longer travel, because I had two knee replacements and used a walker. It was difficult. So they set up a Legacy site. In that way, they set it up so that I could still be a part of the foundation board whenever I felt like attending for the rest of my life.

If you're involved with a university for as long as I've been with Ohio State, which is now 83 years, it's definitely a part of your life, especially when your husband played football there. My husband raised lots of money, including 10 million dollars for the Woody Hayes Hall. I have a wonderful Early Child Education Center there that I just received $13,350,000 grant for over the next five years from the federal government. That money will help improve Head Start in 4200 homes in central Ohio. I have PhDs developing programs there, not for three year olds to five year olds, but from zero to five year olds. We start teaching them when they are infants. Children learn more in the first five years of their life, than at any other time in their life. We're teaching Chinese to children who are three to five years old.

You can't give back at Ohio State, you give forward. You can't give back, because the people that gave to you are gone. You give forward to the university. Woody Hayes started that—giving forward. My husband and I were friends with Woody Hayes. A lot of people may not know this, but Woody was an authoritarian and taught classes on the Civil War. Off season, he taught the Civil War and he was sought by people from all over the United States for lectures. When he had a heart attack, he had no business coming back to football. He got so upset at games. That's when he stopped that boy on the sidelines and he was chastised for it. He was a big believer in education for boys. He wanted them to stay in school and graduate with a degree. Woody is someone I absolutely respect. And he's still respected.

A Simpler Time. ...

It was a simpler time. Life was much simpler. Alex gave me his fraternity pin. That just meant, "I want to go steady with you." And that's the symbol of going steady—the fraternity pin. I think when he asked, it was at Mirror Lake. There's a lake on campus, in the middle of campus on the oval. I think we were standing on a little high point there. And he sang

Getting an Education, Ohio State, & Meeting Alex

me a song. He had a beautiful voice—he could have been an opera singer if he hadn't been a football player. And the song was, "I reach for you, like I reach for the stars." (Singing) "I reach for you like I reach for the stars, worshipping you from a far, when I'm living with my silent love." I remember. I can still see him singing that song. I sure can. It brings tears to my eyes even today.

Those were beautiful days. They were simple. They used to say that you used to spoon. And that's what we did back then.

Hell, yes, I was an old-fashioned girl.

We couldn't go to places, because Alex was working his way through school. He didn't have a lot of money. Oh, we would go to the fraternity and sorority houses and talk. My first year, we were just friends for a couple of years. We studied at the library together. And that library now is glass and you can see all the way down, all the books and shelves. Anyway, I don't like the new library because you can't talk to each other. When we were going there, we would go behind the stacks of books and sneak a little kiss. (Laughs)

It was very difficult because he had football practice and was waiting on tables, so he was busy and he was the BMOC … Big Man on Campus. He was honorary as sophomore, junior, and senior and was very active in the campus organizations. Alex was amazing.

We just grew on each other, because we got to be friends. He started taking me out when I came back to school. After that summer, he visited me at my parent's home. I knew him quite well, because we had been friends for two years. When I announced to mother and daddy that he proposed to me, my mother said, "Why would you marry a dumb football player?" I'm not kidding you. She liked Alex, but she thought all he could do was play football. She didn't realize all the things that he had done in college outside of football. She didn't see the great things that this boy had inside of him. But I did. I saw something in Alex. Something good. That doesn't make me a genius—just lucky and blessed. And I guess a little smart.

Chapter 7

Making a Buck, from Autos to Insurance

"I'm lucky in having found the perfect partner to spend my life with."

—Sara Paretsky

Me and Alex, we didn't talk about the future. One thing I do remember, once when we were driving to Columbus after we got married. We saw a beautiful little home complex on a big piece of land outside the city limits. We found out that it was for sale for $25,000. This is back in 1940. So I said to Alex, "Oh my God, you're making $10,000 a year. We could own a home like this someday, as soon as you really get started on your career. All you have to make is $25,000 a year and we could live comfortably the rest of our lives." It was at times like that when we talked about the future.

There was never an ultimatum to get married—because I forced him to marry me. (Smiles)

He was a traveling salesman and I decided I didn't want to marry a traveling salesman. I knew he was far more capable, because when we were in school, whenever we'd have a prom, he was in charge of the concession stand. He was always making that extra dollar. I remember one night, I came in to a dance with a little dress with hoop skirt, and he said, "You're engaged to me. You can't dance with anybody else." So I stood in the corner and I didn't dance with anybody else. Then he said to me, "Look, don't stand in the corner, come over here to the cash register and watch the ten dollar bills." (Laughs) Watch over the $10 dollar bills, so that no one would take them. Tommy Dorsey had played at that prom and I loved his music, but I didn't get to dance to it. So on my husband's 80th birthday, in Charleston West Virginia, I hired the remnants of the Tommy Dorsey Band and their top singer who was still with them. She sang for over 200 people that I invited to the party. That was Alex's last birthday party. Sadly Alex passed away before his 81st birthday.

So back to the prom—my dance card was empty. He wouldn't let me dance, but I wasn't angry—I was in love.

Let me tell you about how I "forced" Alex to marry me.

It was my parent's anniversary and they were sitting having a portrait taken by the photographer, when he came in to the event. Alex was standing, watching us get the picture taken and I was looking over at him. I was going to say, "You know you got out of school in June. This is March." I was thinking that I would have to give him an ultimatum.

Other boys were calling me for dates, not knowing that I was engaged. One man owned 340 shoe shops and he was from far-away St. Louis, Missouri. He would fly in just to talk with me, but I discouraged him, because Alex would have gotten jealous. He was a very jealous man, my husband. So I was thinking to myself, *You know, I think he's going to do this for the* rest of his life. He's just going to keep dreaming about making a million dollars in one year, but it's never going to happen.

So we went out to dinner that night and afterwards, came to my house. And I said, "Alex, I love you so dearly, but you're not going anywhere. You're standing still, living in the YMCA in Columbus, Ohio. You have a truck, but you don't have a car. You'll be driving around in that truck for the rest of your life." He says, "I make a lot of money."

I replied, "But, Alex, you're not making enough money to support a wife." He said, "But I will, because I'm going to put out advertising. Brylcreem has 'A little dab'll do you' signs all along the roads advertising their product. I'm going to do that, too. I'm going to talk to the man who invented this dandruff product and tell him that I will put up billboards to promote his product, if I can take a percentage of each bottle I sell."

So Alex did talk to the pharmacist, but he said, "Alex, I'm not sure I should tell you this, but the reason my dandruff remover is so good is that there's a little arsenic in it. Remember Cleopatra—she used arsenic in her hair and she had this glorious hair. So when I created my formula, I put a little arsenic in it. That's why I'm not so sure I should be advertising it on the road." Alex replied, "Why didn't you tell me this? I can't promote this product." And he quit.

Well, he calls me up to tell me all this and I said, "Alex, I hate to run your life, but here's what I want you to do. You're going to stay at the YMCA and get a job selling used and new cars or whatever—I don't care what you sell, but you're going to stay in Columbus, Ohio, and you're going to find something where you can make a living."

He said, "Where will we live?" It was April and I said, "As soon as you get back to Columbus and school is out, you find us an apartment that you can rent out by the year, find out how much it will cost—this is what you're going to do. Preferably I would like to be up at Ohio State, because I want to take some classes in science so that I can get my degree." So he quit his job and went to look for an apartment. We rented a furnished efficiency about three blocks from the university for $40 dollar a month.

Four weeks later on a Sunday night, I was married at the Biltmore Hotel in Dayton. It was a beautiful wedding. I didn't even have time to get a white dress. My mother told me that I can't wear white, because my sister isn't married, so I wore a blush pink satin dress. After our beautiful wedding, we went to the Naval Academy for our honeymoon, because Alex's brother was a cadet at the Naval Academy. He was becoming an officer at West Point in Annapolis and couldn't come to the wedding, so we went there to see him.

My husband had borrowed $300 to buy my wedding ring from friends who gave it to him at a good price. You know he was an important football player and he was Jewish and these people were Jewish, so they gave him a good price. When we were on our honeymoon, he told me that he had borrowed the money. I stated, "We're not going to start out our lives together with a debt. I'm taking this ring back and asking them for the money."

I asked him, "Do you think they'll take the ring back?" He said, "I don't know. You could try. But I don't want you taking the ring back."

Making a Buck, from Autos to Insurance

"Well," I said, "I am. I'm not going to be in debt." So I took it back and then went to a 10 cents store and bought a sterling silver ring for one dollar. I wore that ring for five years during the war.

Anyway, Alex had been declared Four F, because he had been kicked in the back playing football. The injury did something to his spine. When we were moving into another apartment, he leaned over one day and he couldn't get up for three weeks until they got him an iron brace (no plastic back then), so he could stand up. He had to keep it with him, because sometimes when he leaned over, it would catch again. Next, he received a commission in the navy as an Ensign in Intelligence. His brother called him from the Naval Academy, "I don't know how you got that. Did you tell them about your brace?" He said, "Well I don't need it all the time." His brother said, "But you need to take it with you, because they won't let you do that. They'll give you an honorable discharge. You get out of that right away." So Alex told them and they classified him as 4F.

We were living in a small apartment that had a living room with a table where we ate, a Murphy bed, a bathroom, and a kitchen—not more than 500 square feet. He wouldn't let me get a job, because his mother never worked, so he didn't think I should work. I wanted to get a job at Lazarus modeling like I did in college, but he wouldn't let me do it. He was a very strong person—**very** strong.

So Alex started selling used cars. He was so good, he got a job with Harry Mellman selling Pontiacs. Harry thought so much of his ability to sell cars that he gave him a job on the floor. He was a great salesman.

When Alex got on the floor in June, Pacific Mutual Insurance heard about his good salesmanship and went over to Pontiac to see him. They asked if wanted to get into the program learning insurance. Alex was interested, so he learned the insurance business and went into it in September of that year. By the following June, he had sold a million dollars of life insurance, which back in 1940 was a *lot* of money. Alex was invited to the National Convention at Sun Valley, Idaho. The wives were not invited, because they just wanted the men come to this convention. That's the first time I was separated from him.

Soon after that, his brother was drafted into World War II. His other brother was in college and played basketball at Ohio State. All four boys were good athletes. The following June, the boys couldn't go home and run their father's bowling business in Charleston, West Virginia.

After about one year in the insurance business, Alex was doing so well, he was offered a partnership in an older man's business. The owner wanted someone to take over, so he wouldn't have to work so hard. However, Alex couldn't accept the partnership, because his older brother was taken in the first draft, so he had to quit his job of managing his father's bowling alleys, which included both a duck pin alley and a regular alley. Alex's father was ill, so he had to go to a California resort to get well. He suffered with angina, so he could not run the bowling alley business anymore. If we didn't go to Charleston and run it, they would lose their family business.

Making a Buck, from Autos to Insurance

By this time, we had a new apartment with all new furniture—everything a person could ask for, and I was going to school for my two science classes, but I had to quit school. We packed up all our new furniture and put it in storage in the hopes that we would go back to Columbus. We traveled to Huntington, West Virginia, in June 1942 and Alex ran the bowling alley.

Because his mother was living in this house by herself, we moved in with her. Thank God, she was a lovely lady. We were there for a couple of years, which I didn't really like at first. Huntington was one of the hell holes of the United States—coal miners, contaminated water, pollution in the air, everything. It was the chemical center of the United States at the time and everything was going in the river. Well, after that, we did live in Charleston, which was the capital and more sophisticated and filled with a lot of lawyers and bright people.

So Alex saved the family business and then in 1942, they built a beautiful brand new bowling alley in Charleston, West Virginia.

We lived there from 1941 to 2013 and just recently sold our home. It was a ranch house that we built on a big lot in 1950, with a river in the back and a river bank with a beautiful hill across from us, with a lot of trees up the rock side. Eventually an interstate was built across from me, but I had trees to block the view, so it didn't bother me.

We wanted to stay in Columbus, but we ended up living in West Virginia for part of the year for 71 years. We split our time staying in West Virginia for three months and Florida nine months, because Emily was in school and we didn't want to take her in and out of school.

In time, I learned to love West Virginia. It's the most beautiful state in the union. The mountains are no higher than 6,000 feet and are forested with the most wonderful woods. When you look down from the sky at West Virginia, it looks like heads of broccoli. It's a gorgeous state with beautiful wildflowers. I was an Ohio girl in my heart, but in time, I learned to love that wonderful little state of West Virginia.

Sometimes in life—actually many times—you don't know where the road will take you. You must have an open mind and heart, and be ready to move to follow your dreams. Alex and I were on the move.

Part Two

Making Our West Virginia Home

Chapter 8

Huntington & Charleston, West Virginia

"Your big opportunity may be right where you are now."

— Napoleon Hill

As World War II raged in Europe, the young couple was again on the move, traveling to West Virginia to help Alex's family out and run a bowling alley. At the time, the average bowler spent under two bucks a week to knock down some pins; gas was cheap at 15 cents a gallon; buying a new car cost about $900 dollars; a loaf of bread dented your pocketbook for under a dime; and a gallon of milk cost you 60 cents. You could buy a home for under $7,000 dollars and if you wanted to send your folks back home a letter, a stamp set you back three pennies. Those things you could budget for, save up for, and count on. The future, well, that was something else altogether—for all Americans. As the war was fought abroad, an outcome was uncertain as a madman named Hitler pushed his evil doctrines, the future for the young couple was uncertain, too. They knew two things: that they loved each other and they were heading to West Virginia—changing lanes both on the highway and in the bowling alleys. With Alex's father recovering, Alex and Betty traveled to the town of Charleston, West Virginia, to run the family's new bowling alley.

What the young couple didn't know yet was how important this move would be for all their futures. And how, with a little imagination, a lot of promotion, and (of course) a lot of perspiration, too—that stuff that Thomas Edison insisted on when predicting success—they would be on the cusp of starting another business of their own, one centered around food and not bowling pins. But for now, they were just another young newlywed couple on the move, with the past in their rearview mirror and everything that life could offer them down the road.

We moved to Huntington to live with Alex's mother.

During the war years, they had built a new bowling alley in Charleston. My father-in-law was feeling better and able to run his bowling alley in Huntington, so we went to Charleston and ran the new bowling alley.

While Alex was doing that, his father took him to the corner of the bowling alley where they had a beautiful V-shaped lot and he said to him, "Alex, I'm going to rent this to the gas station for $300 a month." Alex said, "You know Pop, I've been looking to get into the drive-in food business and I'll give you $400 a month to rent this lot for a year. If I don't make a success of it, you can have it back and give it to the gas station for $300 a month." His father said, "What do you know about the food business?" He said, "Pop, the main thing about business is promotion. If you give them good food, good service, quality food, and you promote it, that's what the restaurant business is all about."

So my husband opened his first drive-in-restaurant in 1947, in Charleston, West Virginia. The name of the restaurant was called the *Parkette*, because you would park and you give them your order.

At this time, with his confidence growing, Alex told his father, "If I don't do a $100,000 there in one year of business, you can have it for the gas station."

People ate in their cars on trays that were clipped to the side of the door. Alex opened the drive-in, because it was cheaper than opening a full service restaurant. He paid $2500 to build the building and $7500 for the equipment. But here is where Alex was really smart and innovative. He put a radio station on top of the restaurant. At the post where you ordered your food, he put a microphone so that you could talk to the people up in the radio station and request the song that you liked played on the radio.

Alex was a great promoter. In six months, he did $200,000 of business! And that's selling 25¢ double-deck hamburgers, French fries, and nickel Cokes. These double-deckers were triple-sliced buns with two meat patties, tomato, lettuce, and cheese if desired, complete with a special sauce, which was a secret formula. He promoted this sandwich called the *Big Boy*, because he was an All-American football player, so everybody called him a big boy. That's how our business started.

In six months, we had to tear down the restaurant and build a bigger one. The new building had a counter with 12 seats. The car hops wore roller skates and uniform like costumes. Every month the car hops would wear a different costume depicting a different foreign country.

Alex was a great promoter.

But this was only the beginning. It was an exciting time and the start of much bigger things to come for all of us. On the horizon, the future looked bright and we were right at the beginning of starting a very large restaurant chain.

Chapter 9

Shoney's

"The entrepreneur always searches for change, responds to it, and exploits it as an opportunity."

— Peter Drucker

Originally we named the restaurant, *Parkette,* because it was a drive-in. Then motorcycles started finding us and you would be sitting there eating in your car and they would zoom around the lot, so we stopped having big parking lots to prevent this. That's when we transitioned into the coffee shop concept and decided to rename the restaurant, because *Parkette* meant you parked and ate.

Since we were changing the name, we decided to have a contest to help rename the restaurant. At the beginning of the contest, I said to my husband, "I have the name that you're going to pick, I just know it."

Alex said, "We're going to get thousands of entries. How can you pick? We're going to give a Lincoln Continental away to the person who names it. How can you say you have the name?" So I said to Alex, "We're going to call it Shoney's." He said, "Why would I call it Shoney's?" I said, "They call your daddy Shoney, right? And they call you Shoney?" He said, "Yes, they do." And I said, "After you get all these names from the contest, you'll find that is the name, the one that no one has ever registered." I said, "S-H-O-N-E-Y." He said, "It's S-C-H-O-E-N-E-Y." I said, "Alex, that could be pronounced - *SC-HO- EENEY* or *SHOW- EENY*, but Shoney's says *SHONEY'S*, so you have to drop the C and spell it SHONEY'S."

I actually picked the name out. The prize for naming it was new Lincoln car. To avoid a conflict of interest, I didn't win the Lincoln. But one man did send in the name of SCHOENY'S so we gave the car to him. This man had the nearest name to Shoney's. I disqualified myself. I didn't want people to say, "She picked out the name ahead of time and then they gave it to her." We had to be able to register the name from all the names we received from the contest to rename the drive-in. Most of the names that we were given, like *The Galaxy*, for example, were not names you could register, because someone may have had the name already. I remember driving that new Lincoln over to give it away to the man who lived in an apartment building.

What happened after we gave him the car now many years later is funny. When I go back to Charleston, maybe 50 people will tell me that their uncle, or their brother or their cousin came up with the name, Shoney. Today everybody's laying claim. (Laughs) None of them know about the lady behind the curtain. Me.

The name had nothing to with Alex's father although his father was known as Shoney at the bowling alley. It was just a good name even if our name wasn't Schoenbaum. Shoney's was a good name. It has that pretty S and H in the beginning and ends with a Y and S. It's an easy name on a sign.

We went from *The Parkette* to Shoney's at that original site. Eventually we closed all the drive-ins ten years after we started them. Drive-ins were the cheapest way to go to get into business back then.

When we opened that first restaurant, I had two boys within the first 14 months, so I was pretty busy. I was not involved in the business. The only thing my husband allowed me to do was the interior decoration of the places. Back in the 1940s, interior decorating wasn't what it is today.

Regarding the theme conveyed at the restaurants, the Big Boy was the most important thing featured. The Big Boy was a statue about seven or eight feet tall of a young boy with red-and-white checkered pants. His hair had a big black cowlick and he was holding a tray that had a double-decker hamburger on it.

Regarding the nomenclature, there are only two Big Boys around and that's because David Frisch decided that he was going to design his own Big Boy. Originally, what happened was we didn't have the Big Boy in our first three restaurants. Then in 1951, we got a letter from Bob Wian in California, who told us that we couldn't use the name because he had registered it. So my husband met him at the National Restaurant Association meeting, which they held every year in May. He met him in Chicago and talked him into franchising. He had kiosks instead of restaurants. I believe he had six kiosks in Glendale, California, where he served Big Boys, French fries, Strawberry Pie, and drinks. My husband said, "If you franchise, we'll pay you a fee and it won't be a small fee." So Bob Wian agreed to franchise and he asked my husband, "What territory do you want?" Alex ended up taking 11 states in the southeast part of the United States. The funniest thing is Alex didn't want Florida, because in those years it was swampland with mosquitoes. He also didn't want Kentucky, Indiana, or Ohio. He wanted to be deeper in the south, part of the contiguous United States. Dave Frisch asked for Florida. Dave Frisch met them at that convention and was part of the group that started the chain, too. He had a different-looking Big Boy that was not as effective as ours. It's like he's walking and he's not carrying a hamburger.

In my husband's region, he had Virginia, North and South Carolina, Georgia, Tennessee, Louisiana, Alabama, and Arkansas, which we moved into later. He also had rights to anything north of that, like Baltimore, but my husband didn't want to go that far north. We also had some restaurants in Philadelphia and Boston, where people asked for our franchise.

At this time, Alex is working hard—he was a workaholic. Me, I'm sort of laid back and I had two babies to raise with no help, because we were putting all of our money into the business. I had two boys 14 months apart.

It was quite a journey from *The Parkette* to the first Shoney's. We were the third restaurant franchise in the United States. A&W was the first franchise, Howard Johnson's was the second and the third one was Big Boy. McDonald's and Colonel Sanders weren't in business yet.

The restaurant business was a big part of our lives, from

1947 to 1996, when my husband died. Alex truly was an icon in the restaurant business. He was a trailblazer and I remember when he got this award, some wonderful china boots that he received. They were from Multi-Unit of Food Service Operators of the United States. You had to have multi-units and own a chain. He was awarded this in 1984. It says Alex Schoenbaum, Shoney's.

Some of the other people on that list who received the award are Colonel Sanders, (Harlan Sanders), J. Willard Marriott from Marriott, and Ray Kroc who started McDonalds, but they got their awards earlier than we did, even though we were in business longer than they were.

When he started, Colonel Sanders was killing his chickens in the barn behind his home—he'd just gotten in business and was doing really good. In fact, he had an interior decorator do his farmhouse—he felt so proud that he could afford an interior decorator. She had to come from Cincinnati, because there were no interior decorators in Selbyville, Kentucky. Oh, I could tell you stories.

We knew Harlan Sanders personally—in fact, he came to my husband when Alex started his chain. Sanders asked him to come and work for him, because he wasn't a youngster when he got into business. The Colonel was nice man, a very nice country gentleman, but my husband told the Colonel that he wanted to be his own boss.

That award was a big honor. Especially when you see some of the recipients who have been honored, like Colonel Sanders or Marriott, which is a huge corporation. We bought their stock, which has split many times since we got them. In fact, we sold them a couple of our companies, and even sold them the Shoney's franchise. Marriot was $9 and now it is $89. I read the statement every month when I read about my stocks. I keep involved in everything I give to as well, as I do in everything that pertains to me in terms of business.

While we sought our *American Dream,* we were able to produce something so we could give something back. While I didn't work in the business, I did influence Alex. He wrote a column in his corporate newspaper that went out to his employees. Sometimes in the newspaper, Alex would cover subjects that we talked about, such as the welfare of the world. The newspaper also served as a vehicle that would lift our employee's spirits, while giving us a chance to thank them for their devotion, loyalty, and being so dedicated.

In fact, whenever he wrote a column in his paper, it was often about something he and I had discussed. Alex didn't tell me when he was going to put my words in his column, and then I read it, only to realize he had put my words in the newspaper.

He was skillful with everyone as an employer. The relationship between an employer and employee is a two-way street and relationship, with each party doing his part. Employer to employee and employee to employer, they owed each other something.

In Alex's world, the employee owed the employer *Honesty.* Don't steal from the employer. Like one time, an employee said he was taking the bread out to feed the chickens. On the way to his car, he stumbled and fell. A great big ten-pound ham had been lodged under his coat—a big one—a huge ham

Shoney's

that he was trying to sneak out to his home. So my husband called his employees together in a meeting and said, "You have to let me make money or I can't pay you. If you steal from me, I'm not going to be able to pay you, and you will all be losing your jobs—all of you. From now on, you cannot leave here without the manager checking out what you are taking home."

Alex felt that the employer owed his employees the same thing. *Honesty.* The same thing. *Integrity and Honor.* His motto was, "If you have wonderful service, you have good employees and your food is good, you can't miss. And not only that, your food has to be top-notch quality."

There we so many big names there when he received this award. One person in this shot, his name is Carl Karcher. He founded a little drive-thru chain called Carl's Jr. Many of the people on this list who've gotten awards already, such as Jim McLamore of Burger King, Robert Wian of Bob's Big Boy, William Rosenberg of Dunkin Donuts, and Dave Thomas of Wendy's were all there. Dave Thomas was a wonderful man, an orphan who was adopted by a great family. It was quite important to be honored at this event as the fourth recipient. When Alex got up and received the award, I almost burst with pride.

Back in the day, I would visit all the Shoney's down south. I would meet Alex in these different places and then, we'd meet the governors of the state. I remember they picked me up in New Orleans with a motorcycle escort that took me to the hotel. Big limousine and flowers. The people thought I was some important person. I put on sunglasses so they wouldn't

The Joy of Giving is the Joy of Living

see that it was just a little old lady in the back seat. Visiting all these places was a wonderful experience. So many memories.

I was looking in a book and thinking about when we put in our coffee shop. Marriot had bought the franchise from the five owners of the franchise, who were already operators. They had bought the franchise from the man who owned it originally for Big Boy.

Bill Marriot, THE Bill Marriot, came to Charleston many times and he also came to Ohio State when they dedicated the undergraduate School of Business - Schoenbaum Hall. They had a big dinner at Les Wexner for 100 people and one of the people in attendance was Max Fischer who gave 25 million dollars to the Max Fisher School of Business. Also at the event was his best friend, Gerry Ford. So at what table did I sit? I thought I was going to sit with all my children who had come for the dedication. Instead they sit me between Gerry Ford and Max Fisher. I'm thinking to myself, "What am I going to talk about with these people? I don't know about politics. I know Democrat. I know Republican, I know who's important but I don't know them." And so we sat down, and Gerry Ford and I started talking. His spoke about his wife who was a dancer. Well, I had studied dance and had danced in New York. So we talked about dancing. The next thing we talked about was football. He was an All-American at Michigan and my husband was an All-American at Ohio State—so we talked about football. Then we talked about our kids—his kids, my kids. We had a great time. What a nice man—even if he was a Michigan fan. (Smile) It was a friendly confrontation between a Buckeye and a Wolverine. Oh my

Shoney's

God, we had a ball together. Really had a good time. At the time Max Fisher was one of the most important people in the Republican Party in the entire United States. I believe he made his money with the first automatic gas pump, where you could put gas in your own tank at the gas station. Max came from Ohio State and he played football there in 1931.

I was perfectly comfortable. We three talked. The whole table wasn't talking. I don't even remember the other people at the table. I'm sure the president of the university was there, who I knew, but I don't remember anyone else. Gerry Ford was a lovely, lovely man.

I sometimes think, "Is there a thread inherent in someone becoming successful?" It used to be hard work, dedication, and focus to your business. And another thing, there used to be integrity. It's gone. It's gone from the top down. My husband's motto was, "You give them the finest quality food you can buy. You give it to them at decent prices so that you can make a buck and they can get good food, and they get good service, good recipes, and you can make it."

Alex was busy with the business and I had my kids. Until 66, I had a child at home. I was cooking dinner every night. But I ate at Shoney's a lot. They had a wonderful salad bar. A *big* salad bar. And it was cheap—$6.95. Alex was innovative and was the first one to introduce salad bars in restaurants.

Whatever the restaurant business is, it's a tough business. It's a tough business. I mean, how many hamburger places can you have? To be good and sustainable, Alex had his formula: Quality food. Good Chefs. Good Service. You can't miss.

Of all the Shoney's, I think my favorite one is on the

boulevard in Charleston. It's the only one that's left in Charleston, West Virginia. There used to be eight, right around Charleston. I guess it was my favorite, because I knew all the waitresses. Some of them had been working there forty or fifty years. I'd take my kids there. My kids worked there.

My kids learned the restaurant business by scraping gum off the parking lot—a nickel a wad. It wasn't hard work. Alex taught them the business the right way. He felt it was important that they know every facet of the business and they would have no problems.

He was right. Alex was always right on the business and he worked so hard. Sometimes when I think back to how he started with one little place and built it into something so big, I'm even amazed. Wow!

Chapter 10

Married to an Entrepreneur

"There is nothing in the world like the devotion of a married woman. It is a thing no married man knows anything about."

— Oscar Wilde

My husband was a believer that women should not work and that they should stay at home with their kids, just like his mother did.

Women didn't work back then. They stayed home and took care of their children, even during the depression, because there weren't jobs for women that warranted them going out and working. During those years, becoming a teacher, secretary, nurse, or a maid were the only jobs or professions that were available to women.

Well, the good side of it was that we did take care of our children. Our children had wonderful childhoods, because the mama was home. Women like me, if you wanted to become active, you became active in your church or temple or you became active in organizations in the town.

And that's what I did. I got involved with the Boys Scouts

and the Girl Scouts. Everything. I'd go to the Sunday School. I'd be cooking. Eventually, when I had two daughters, I became the cookie chairman of the Girl Scouts and my house would be full of cookies.

I saw no negatives to this at all, because my mother had done the same thing. I think we gave our children a balanced life. Our home life was very busy. Alex never liked to eat out at night. Having been a restaurant owner, he wanted to eat dinner every night at home. Alex wanted me to cook and I cooked. All I know is that I gave him balanced meals. I would make an appetizer, an entrée, a starch, a vegetable, and a soup. I loved to make soup. It was a non-fattening diet, because my husband was a little on the heavy side. He was very big-boned and couldn't find a hat to fit him, because his head was so big and he couldn't find gloves to fit him, because his hands were so big. He couldn't find shoes—even Tom McCann only carried up to size 12, and my husband wore a 14D. He was a big boy.

I remember those days with him. We had some exciting days. We'd go on tours of the south. They would meet me at the airport with the limousine and a police escort to take me to my hotel. We were going to restaurant conventions and openings, so my parents would come down from Dayton to take care of the children. For me it was normal, because my own daddy went to work and my mother stayed home.

My husband was an overachiever, who had ADD before they knew what it was. Alex was a good football player and I remember him telling me how the coaches begged the teachers to keep him eligible, because he was All-State both as a junior and senior in high school. They didn't care if he was getting his education or not. When he got to his senior year, they found he didn't have enough credits to graduate high school. His father got him a scholarship to Kiskiminetas Springs Prep School in Pennsylvania, which formerly was the Kiski School, a prep school for football players in the Pittsburgh area who were going to the local university. That's where he would have gone, but then Ohio State offered him a scholarship and he decided to go to there.

He flunked his first year at KISKI on purpose, because for the first time in his life, he was learning. He never had to learn before that. Alex just kept being promoted to the next grade. People with ADD are bright people, but their brains are different than other people, and because of that, when they find something that they love—my husband loved that business—they excel way beyond other people, because of their concentrated focus. That was a plus for him eventually.

Our lifestyle was changing. We are living in Charleston, West Virginia, in a $15,500 house that was very nice. When my boys were 12 and 13, we built a beautiful home on the river in Charleston. But up to that time, we lived in a three-bedroom home, with one bath on the second floor and a powder room on the first floor. It was nice home with a family room downstairs. We built that lovely home in Charleston on the river in 1959 and stayed there until 2014. I had my two boys, Raymond and Jeffry, and then my Joann was born when I was 39. Unexpectedly, at 48½ years of age, I had a BIG surprise when my daughter Emily was born.

We went from a small apartment to a nice home to a

bigger home. I didn't take anything for granted. I just think how blessed I am. People have asked what my life has been like and I tell them, "I have lived a blessed life all my life—all of my life." And you know that I have a word for my life—ineffable, a joy beyond description. And I'm still living it.

When the wives are working, something is missing in that dynamic. What is missing is family life. There is nothing like family life. A lot of people give their children material things to make up for the fact that they're working and everything. Still, I feel it doesn't compensate for a mother not being able to be at home with her children.

In life you go by what you have seen as a model. My mother was a wonderful mother, so she stayed home. Most women stayed home then. That wasn't different back then—it was the norm. I was happy, ineffable joy. I've had a beautiful life. My boys were involved in athletics and my daughters were involved in dancing and music

It was a busy life with three children and growing the business. We traveled a little bit, but not a lot. We didn't travel when the kids were still at home, but waited until they started going to college. And then when Emily came, we just took Emily with us when we traveled. She had a different life than the other children, because nobody was at home with her. In fact, my boys really never did get to know their sister after they graduated college. They were in college when she was born and lived in Atlanta, Georgia, when they got out of college.

It's been a busy and a full life. It's unimaginable for me what my life would have been like without my family and the ability to become a mother.

Chapter 11

Mother's Day with All My Children

*"Pregnancy and motherhood are the most
beautiful and significantly life-altering events that
I have ever experienced."*

— Elisabeth Hasselbeck

It is something that Betty strongly believes in. This concept called motherhood. This love and duty of being a mother—something she inherited from both her mother, Sarah, and her grandmother, Fanny, both of whom had four children each.

Following in their footsteps, she emulated them not only in her love for motherhood, but also in the fact that she had four children of her own.

I feel blessed that I just finished another Mother's day celebration with all my children.

I didn't have all my grandchildren there, but my children will be with me this weekend again for the tribute to Alex, where Urban Meyer will be honored by Dick Vitale, who is such a wonderful man. He gives not only of his time, but also of his money to help children fighting cancer.

I want to talk about the qualities that best describe my children.

I have four children.

Starting with Raymond, he's the oldest, who was born when I was 28 years old and who is now 72. How fortunate am I to see my children arrive at the age of 70. It's a blessing. A true blessing.

My children are exact opposites. I have two boys and two girls. Two of them who love to spend money on clothes, homes, and whatever they want, and I have two that don't find that important.

When my husband passed away, I did give each of my children enough money so that they could buy themselves a gorgeous home, because I felt like, "Why should I wait until I die to give it to them? I'll give it now, so I can go and enjoy it." They could have quarters for grandma, for nana at their house, and I could come in and enjoy their family, but not be a bother.

Ray is the oldest and not only is he carefree, but he believes in buying the best and enjoying it. His attitude is, "If you run out of money, you run out of money." But thank God, he was very successful in life and he could afford every cent he spends.

He's a conservative me. I'm a conservative Raymond. I buy what I want to buy, because I like beautiful things and I enjoy them. Raymond believes in enjoying what he has and I see nothing wrong in that.

Raymond's the only one out of the four that built the beautiful house that I wanted them to build. He has a suite for me, separate from the rest. When I go there, I'm treated like a

Mother's Day with all My Children

queen—my own room and bath, near the kitchen, so everything is very convenient.

Raymond always wanted to go into business with his father. He attended college at Denver University where he played football. Football was so important there. He played football in school and went away to prep school his last two years of high school. He wanted to go to the same prep school that his daddy went to—the Kiski School, formerly the Kiskiminetas Springs School, near Pittsburgh. Raymond also had ADD and felt more comfortable going to prep school for two years to get more attention from the teachers. At the University of Denver, Raymond went to a restaurant and hotel school and earned his four-year degree there. Having gone to a small prep school, he didn't want to go to a big hotel/restaurant school.

It's quite an amazing story when you think of it—the growth of my husband's business. When Raymond got out of college, his father told him that that he had a location and asked if he wanted to open up a Shoney's. Raymond said yes, but that he would like to go to Atlanta. His daddy said, "You can live in Atlanta, but this store I want to open up is in Rome, Georgia." So Raymond opened up a Shoney's in the little town of Rome with only 15,000 people. At that time, we had about 350 restaurants, which grew to be 2,016 restaurants in 36 states.

One weekend, Raymond came home and while we were having breakfast, he wanted to crow about his success. "Daddy, what do you think about your son? I'm number 13 out of all the restaurants in the chain in sales. Isn't that great?" His daddy said, "Oh hell, with what I taught you, you ought to be in the top ten if not number one."

Here was this big 6'5' boy that is my son, with tears in his eyes. He came into the kitchen from the breakfast room, where I was doing the dishes and said, "Mom, am I ever going to satisfy and please my father?" I turned to him and said, "You don't live your life to please your father. Raymond, if you are, stop right now. This is not a life—you should satisfy yourself. You're happy about what you are doing, and proud of it, and you are making a lot of money. You go sell that store and with money that you make on that, you go and get yourself a franchise that your daddy thinks is really hot right now—it's Wendy's. It's just starting in Columbus, Ohio."

Raymond and a partner soon decided to do their own thing, just as I had advised him. "No matter what you do with your father, he's never going to be pleased. He's always going to want more from you. You are very capable, so you go out and start what *you* want to do." Then I asked him, "What do you want to do?" Raymond said, "Well I've always wanted to own a fine dining restaurant."

And that's exactly what he ended up doing very successfully. But first, Raymond achieved great success in opening a number of Wendy's restaurants. Next, he turned his attention to opening a chain of 21 Mexican restaurants called *Rio Bravo*. This was hot and one of the early Mexican chains. Sales were terrific. People would sit out with their margaritas and wait for a table for an hour. People loved the restaurant! He opened in Atlanta and in other cities, too and had some in Florida. Eventually he sold them to Applebee's.

With that money, he pursued his dreams of

Mother's Day with all My Children

developing and opening a fine dining restaurant in Atlanta on the Chattahoochee River, called *Ray's on the River*.

After 27 years of renting there, the owner sold him the property, which permitted Raymond to make improvements and develop it into one of the most beautiful restaurants in Atlanta. *Ray's on the River* does very, very well. It has a wonderful location. Sometimes the symphony comes and plays on the river banks. On Mother's Day, they did more business than any restaurant in the city of Atlanta, because of the location and they have outside seating on the riverbank. *Ray's on the River* is a gorgeous modern art deco restaurant, a very fine place to dine.

After selling some of his Applebee's stock, which he received in payment for Rio Bravo, he opened two more restaurants. *Killer Creek Chophouse* in Alpharetta, Georgia, and one on Peachtree, in the middle of Atlanta, called *Ray's in the City*. All three of these restaurants do very well.

Raymond has been very successful in business today and he started with one Shoney's.

I'm proud of him. I'm proud of all my children.

My second child, Jeffry came 14 months after his brother. He turns 70 in 2017. Like Raymond he got involved with a chain of *Wendy's* restaurants.

Jeffry is different from Raymond in that he's very frugal. Material things don't mean a lot to him. He would just as soon buy a second-hand car with 10,000 miles on it and pay $5,000 less, than get the model that they're making now. But that's Jeffry. I admire him for this, too, because his brother goes off the scale the other way. (Laughs)

The Joy of Giving is the Joy of Living

My boys are polar opposites. They're completely different. I could see from their childhood how it happened. Raymond was born with club feet and they put casts on him when he was six weeks old. It happened, because he was 23 inches long and his natal position within me was crowded and his feet got stuck under his knees instead of being folded up like a normal child is inside the womb. He wore those casts until he was two years old. You would never know from about the time he was four years old that he had a problem with his feet. But we catered to Raymond and leaned over backward, because he could not walk so well. As my first born, we handled Raymond differently and then 14 months later, Jeffry was born. In taking care of Raymond who had casts, I spent more time with him and because of that, Jeffry grew up more independent. I was still there for him all the time. I wasn't the kind of mother that ran away. I didn't play bridge or Mahjong. I was a mother. That was my main thing in life.

Jeffry went into the restaurant business, too. He had a chain of Wendy's, which he sold and invested that money wisely many years ago, so he could retire. He lives in a nice Key West home in Palm Harbor, Florida, but it's an older house. They lived in Tampa for a while, but when they retired, they bought The Key West model home from the developer of their community on Lake Tarpon. Raymond lives in Atlanta. They have a boat and my sons enjoy boating together. Both of my boys are good family men.

Both my sons also married well. Raymond married an absolutely wonderful girl. I have so much love for Susan and admire her in so many ways. Nobody has more friends than

Mother's Day with all My Children

Susan Schoenbaum in Atlanta. Strangely enough, Jeffry's wife is also named Susan, so we call her Sue. Sue is a leader. She was a convert to Judaism and was president of Temple Beth Shalom in Sarasota, Florida, and she was the head of the Tampa Jewish Federation for four years. She helped raise 21 million dollars for a new Jewish Community Center in Tampa that they are planning to build.

My daughter Joann is "Miss Personality." When you are with Joann, you have fun. You laugh a lot. She is just great company and is a very attentive daughter. Very attentive to me. She bakes me things and brings food to me. She's afraid that I'm going to starve and Joann loves to shop till she drops.

As far as shopping goes regarding my boys, Raymond buys custom-made suits, while Jeffry buys his Dockers at Sears and Roebuck.

Joann is married to a wonderful, wonderful man, Rick Miller. He's just the dearest person. He reminds me of my father. You never call a man sweet, but they're sweet dear men. They are quieter, but what they say is very important. He's been a good dad and a wonderful husband. He and Joann have a good relationship, which makes me very glad. Joann went through a life-threatening ordeal when a tumor was discovered on her brain. Thankfully it was benign, but it was very difficult to remove. She is a fighter and survived it, and now she's back to normal—that is, as normal as you can be when you approach 60. (Laughs) Joann is truly a delight.

Then there is Emily. Emily came to me when I was 48½ years old. Yes—it was a shock! She was healthy and normal when she was born, thank God. Emily was the most beautiful baby and child. Everybody will tell you that. You can just look at Emily and KVELL. That's a Jewish expression. We were thrilled all over because she was a delight. Very bright and good in school. She earned her Master's Degree in Education at Tulane University.

Emily was in a field where she was responsible for teaching addicted babies, who were now wards of the state, to use their brains. Tragically they were brain-damaged, because they were fed alcohol and narcotics in the womb. While they were weaned away from the drugs, sadly they fried their brains and you could not teach them.

After she left that job, she returned to remodeling a brownstone apartment house for people that come to Washington DC to work in the Embassy and who require some housing. Because housing is so hard to find in Washington DC, these business apartments go fast. They are wired and prepped to do business. They include a bedroom, kitchenette, living room, and a bathroom, but they leased them by the year and she did well.

After living in Washington for many years, she decided to move to New Orleans. While she was at Tulane University, she was on the rowing team there, so she now loves New Orleans. It is home to her really more than Washington ever was. Washington D.C. is a different city when it comes to living. It's very urban.

I hope that Emily finds a companion to live with or marry. She has had a number of relationships, but for various reasons, she tells me that men change after they have been with you for six months and that they are different people.

Mother's Day with all My Children

"Once they think that they've got you, Mother, they're different. They want to be with the guys."

I get so much joy out of my daughter, Emily, that it's just amazing. She's here for me. The minute that she knows I'm in trouble, she's here. She's very concerned about me. Even with all her brothers and sisters and the rest of the extended family, I'm the closest one to her.

I have often said this about my in-laws, my two daughters-in-law, and my son-in-law. "If I stand in a circle and we hold hands, I can feel the love going from one hand to another all the way around the circle." I am really blessed to have that and to be loved. I love them because they put up with my children. You know your children's faults. God bless them all. (Laughs) You ask me my favorite and I have no favorite. I don't have a favorite child.

I don't play favorites. If they have a disagreement, they don't get involved in front of me. I don't see that. I'm a Libra. Libra's are fair. We are balanced. I don't take sides. I've found it best to "just keep my mouth shut."

Especially on days like Mother's Day, I realize I started this whole tree. It makes me realize that all these people in this photo would not have been here had I not married Alex Schoenbaum. You realize how blessed you are. When it's all said and done, it's not about the money that I gave, it's not about the people I helped, what it's all about, is your family.

I'm proud of every one of my four children. They are wonderful citizens and are part of the communities in which they live. They care about other people and are active in helping other people. Fortunately, three of my children are married at this time. My fourth one has never been married. She's beautiful. She's lovely. She's looking for somebody that has the same altruistic ideals that she has and I don't think they make them anymore. What she loves, what she should be is a farmer, she really should. She should live out on farm and grow organic foods. She's an environmentalist and realist. She campaigns for the underprivileged and people who are trod down on, like migrant workers—she works hard for migrant workers. She's pro-abortion and an outspoken liberal. She was a member of Greenpeace, which is an organization that fights the extinction of the environment. She went to Africa and built wells in the villages and a community center. She's a do-gooder. That's Emily. She is very strong like her father. Very strong.

As a person, Raymond is happy. He should have been a lawyer, because if he wanted something bad enough, if you were the parent, you would bend and give it to him. But I never did. When he would argue with me and try to introduce his lawyer personality, I just wouldn't give in to him.

I'm very proud of his business sense. He does a very good job. But because of his ADD, he's a little short when you want to talk to him. He's standing in front of you, but you don't know where his mind is.

Still, my God yes, I'm very proud of him. I know Alex is proud of all our kids. He taught those kids everything that you had to know about running a business.

I tell everybody, I am one of the most blessed women in the world. All three of my children, this is the God's truth, married outstanding people. Outstanding people. I love them, sometimes, more than my children. No, I really do, because they put up with my kids. No, really, I'm not saying that in jest—it's real.

Ray and Susan had two sons, Mark, who is married and has two children, two of my great-grandchildren. And Mark's wife is something else—she wrote a book her senior year of college and it was published. The other son, Brian, was recently mentioned by Forbes magazine as an entrepreneur, and he is forming a Hub in Austin, Texas, where they get a lot of intelligent people together in one building, and all of a sudden, they're forming companies and everything. Now he's going national. He's gorgeous. Gorgeous. He was recently named outstanding bachelor in Austin, Texas.

My Jeffry was the easiest child in the world to raise. You told him to keep his clothes clean—he kept his clothes clean. Raymond couldn't care less. (Laughs) And now Raymond is the one who's the dresser and Jeffry buys his clothes at Sears and Roebuck. Why? He's richer than Raymond and he wants to die richer than his brother. Raymond spends it. Jeffry hoards it.

When Raymond went into Wendy's, Jeffry decided he would also get into Wendy's and he got a wonderful territory—Norfolk, Virginia, and Virginia Beach, Williamsburg, and Portsmouth. He got that whole area for Wendy's. He didn't like the business. Fortunately, his wife, Sue, is a very capable woman and she worked hand-in-hand with him. They had 21 restaurants that they sold back to Dave Thomas and Wendy's like Raymond did. With the money, he went out and bought a lot of real estate in Florida and he's done very well with that. Jeffry has two boys—Jay and Adam.

The Joy of Giving is the Joy of Living

I'm most proud of Jeffry in his life in that I think he has more friends than anybody in the world. Perhaps the reason they achieved so much is that my husband had a habit of challenging my children negatively. Instead of telling them when they had an idea, "Go do it. Try it. If you don't succeed you'll learn something." Alex didn't encourage them that way. He never said that. What he said was, "I bet you can't do it," all the while, he was thinking that they were going to do it for him. You know, that's no good. I told my children, you do it for yourself and not for your daddy.

They all graduated from college, except Jeffry.

He came home from spring vacation from his senior year in school and decided to go straight downtown. There was a wreck on the boulevard that involved Jeffry. There was no stop street and the boulevard was really torn up and lumpy, because we had a terrible winter, so they had to salt all winter. You couldn't speed on the boulevard if you wanted to, because you would tear the bottom out of your car. On this day, Jeffry stopped at Shoney's to get a bite before he went down to the newspaper, where he hoped to find out the basketball scores. At that time, they didn't publish the basketball scores until the morning, so he went to the newspaper to get some scores. On his way downtown, a car was heading down the boulevard and making a left turn at a street and going pretty fast. I guess the driver thought he could make the turn before Jeffry got there with his car. Jeffry saw him slow up, so he went ahead to make the turn, and Jeffry hit his front door on the right-hand side of the car. Two boys were returning to work at the newspaper and he killed the boy. It was not

Jeffry's fault. The police came and said it was absolutely not his fault, saying that Jeffry had the right of away. The boy had no business cutting in front of him. Anyway, whether it was his fault or not, he killed a boy the same age as he was. And he could not get over that. So when we sent Jeffry back to school to get his degree in business, he still had his finals to take yet. He took uppers to wake up and lowers to put himself to sleep. He was on all these drugs, because he couldn't live with it.

Jeffry finally came out of this, but he didn't graduate from college. He never got over it—never got over it. When the sister of the boy who was killed saw him on the street one day, she came up to him and said, "You killed my brother." That really set him off. I don't think he ever forgave himself. Still the boy was killed, even if you forgive yourself.

Sometimes you are in the wrong place at the wrong time. Well I just kept telling him, "Jeffry it was unavoidable, honey, whether it was you or somebody else at the wheel. That same incident would have happened again." I said, "You didn't pull in front of that car. He pulled in front of you. It happened in your lane and there was no stop sign. No stop sign. There never was."

This was in West Virginia. It was the main road in Charleston next to the river in front of the capital and it ran all the way downtown.

Everybody gets cards in life dealt to them. It is how we deal with them that is our plight. Jeffry went on to have good life, even after that. Yes, he's had a good life.

He lives in Palm Harbor and has a boat and alligators in his yard. His son, Adam, lives there and is super-successful.

Both sons. Jay is a successful financial planner living in New Mexico. He is one of the only two that are far away in my family. Jay had a beautiful home in Albuquerque that was 5400 feet high above sea level and then they moved to a little hideaway home that was 7200 feet high altitude. They loved it so much. They have a farm and goats that they have to milk. They have a wonderful life. He has a tractor and the children get on the tractor. They know how to build a dam. He loves the environment, so they're out in the gorgeous mountains. Oh, my God, gorgeous. It kind of reminds me of my cottage days when I was young.

With my first daughter Joann, I had a grandfather named Joe and a grandmother named Anne, so she's Joann. She's number three and it took me ten years to get pregnant with her. I had Jeffry at 29 and I had her at 39.

I always wanted four children. I was raised with four children in my childhood and I had the most delightful childhood, so I wanted to have four so that they could have a wonderful childhood.

I was trying to get pregnant for eight years and every month you wait and you think that you're going to get pregnant. So when you do get pregnant, you don't care if it's a girl, boy, a dog or a cat. And I mean that. As long as it's healthy.

Joann was delightful to raise, truly delightful. She always had a lot of friends. She's got a great personality and was older when she got married. She was working for Coca-Cola, and lived out in Hermosa Beach in California and for a long time was going with this boy who Alex didn't particularly like. I convinced her to go to Tampa. I told her, "Joann, come on back to Sarasota and you can see if he's right for you. If you see each other only four times a year, people change, Joann, remember that." So she came back and saw him for three weeks and broke off with him. Then she went to a Jewish Singles Party and met this shy man, named Richard Miller who became head of the Osteopathic Dermatologists of the United States. Not only that, but he's an angel. She is never wrong with him—even when she's wrong.

They are all married still and that is truly a blessing.

Joann has three girls. Lovely beautiful daughters. Sarah, who lives in Austin now, graduated from Michigan. Lauren is going to be a nurse and she's graduating from the University of Georgia, where she's getting her degree in nursing. And Lindsay is down at Fort Myers at Florida Gulf Coast University, where she is earning straight A's.

All our children are different from the both of us.

I can't spend money like Raymond spends. My husband couldn't spend like that. When my husband wanted a suit, he would park behind the store, have me carry the suits out and if he found one that he liked he would go inside and have it fitted. Otherwise he wouldn't go in. No he didn't like clothes. I'll tell you why. It was hard for him to find clothes the right sizes by the time you get a 48 shoulder, the waist sizes were real big. He had to have all his shirts custom-made, because he had a 20-inch collar and shirts only went up to 17½ back then. His hands and feet were too big. He couldn't find hats, gloves, or shoes to fit him. But I fit him. (Laughs) He sure loved me. He did. He wasn't a person who bubbled over with emotions. But he showered me with respect.

We did great. He had a lot of honor, my husband, integrity and honor. If he gave his word it was gold and if you gave your word to call at 10 am and you called later he would give you hell. His word was his honor. That's from that generation and they need more of that.

Which child takes after me the most? None of them. I came up in the depression and the depression affected you to watch your pennies from then on. I still watch my pennies and cut coupons out of the paper. Sure, if I can pay four dollars less for something I will. I just don't waste money. I try not to.

When I think of all my children, from grand to great, I have said this before, that family is the most important thing to me. I have the most gorgeous family. They're all beautiful inside and outside.

A person's heart and soul. Well that's the most important thing. It's not the façade that you see that's bought by money. It's what is inside that is important.

My family is like that. I'm thanking God right now for all of them. (Tears up) The beautiful part is seeing your grandchildren get married. That, too. That didn't happen when Alex was living. There were no great-grandchildren. Now another baby is going to be born tomorrow.

Another great-grandchild.

Another blessing.

Chapter 12

Blessings & Shock: A Baby at 48

"Nearly all the best things that came to me in life have been unexpected, unplanned by me."

— Carl Sandburg

When I had Emily, I was 48½ years old.

I already had two boys in college, one at Denver University and one at University of Arizona. When they heard I was pregnant, they were proud of me. (Laughs) At that time I had Joann at home who was nine years old. She loved it, because she had prayed for a little sister for years. She got the little sister, so I blamed her for that baby. (Laughs) When you have a child, you are much more active than if you don't have one. I think that helped my health and balanced my hormones. Things are happening to me now that most people have in their late forties.

I was worried sick when I found that I was pregnant. I wondered if I should be pregnant at this age. Of course, I never thought about abortion, because I had always wanted four children. So God gave me my fourth one when I was a little north of 48. I felt wonderful during my pregnancy. When I'm pregnant, I can do anything. In fact, my husband turned 50 right before I found out I was pregnant. His birthday is in August and I found out in September that I was pregnant. I had 40 of his managers at our house and I fixed dinner. I could do anything when I was pregnant. It really revitalized me. I had an eight-pound five-ounce daughter in an hour and twenty five minutes. Healthy, beautiful, and gorgeous.

They don't teach you much after you've had three of them. With the fourth one, you know it all. Even for the first one I wasn't the nervous mother. Now I thought, "This is life."

The boys really didn't know their sister, Emily, simply because they were in college and in the summertime, they would work with their father at the restaurants. They would come for family gatherings, but the relationship was not there between the boys and Emily. They loved Emily and thought she was adorable, but they didn't interact with her too much, because they weren't home.

When I brought Emily home, it was heaven—because I had a baby. I loved babies and she was so beautiful. Oh wow! You should see photos of Emily when she was a baby.

I got involved with Girl Scouts and cookies and that sort of stuff with Emily. I was a Girl Scout leader. In fact, I met one of my Girl Scout's children last night in Sarasota, because she lives in the Sara Bay Club and her children are visiting her. It was so funny to sit and think that when she was 13 years old, she was a Girl Scout of mine. She said to me, "I got the cooking badge. And everybody thinks I'm a good cook." (Laughs) Anyway it was cute. For the Boy Scouts, I was a den mother.

Nine-year-old Joann was not jealous at all. Oh my God, she had prayed for that baby. She adored Emily. And to Emily—this was her life.

At this time, we are in Charleston and are very comfortable financially. When I had my boys, we lived in a one-bedroom apartment. I'll tell you the difference. When I went to the grocery store when the boys were little and I got to the checkout counter, they would grab everything that is enticing to children. I had a terrible time with two kids in the basket. They didn't have the little cars like today. At the time, I never carried anything more than a ten dollar bill, so when I paid the cashier, I would be so distracted by the boys—I would always wonder if I give the clerk a twenty or a ten? And the difference with Emily—well, let me think. I still was pulling ten dollar bills out. I don't feel as far as security that it made any difference. I don't think I bought any more toys for Emily, because I had the money. I brought Emily up like I did the rest of the children, because it was a good formula. I had good kids, so why not do the same?

Alex didn't raise the kids. The business was first. I was the one who raised the children. You teach them what you should teach them. Basics of life. Liking other people and if you can't say something nice about a person, don't say anything. Just the normal things that make a basically good human being.

The only problem that my children have given me is

that their father smoked cigarettes from the time he was 14 years old to the age of 81, which is when he died. Alex was an athlete. A great athlete. He thought he was indomitable and that nothing would happen to him. And my children knowing that their daddy lived to 81, they're opting to smoke. My advice is, "Don't start smoking. It's very addictive, if not the *most* addictive thing out there." I feel that people who smoke don't really like themselves. They know what smoking does to them—they tell you all the time. Yet they continue smoking, because they don't like themselves. That's my conception.

Emily was a good student in school right from the beginning. She was smart. Emily was my smartest child intellectually. Her ability to converse with people is amazing. Emily is liberal and for the downtrodden and she's against what they're doing to the environment. She's been a member of Green Peace and was second in command in Washington at their headquarters. The head of that organization quit and she was in line for a new position, but they brought in a new man, so she left Green Peace because of that. But she did go to Africa during her lifetime and helped with a project in a village, and I think they helped dig wells or build a community center.

She's very philanthropic and a big supporter of Planned Parenthood. She's altruistic. I'm proud of her because she defends the underprivileged. Yes, she's a lot like me. But I'm not a raving liberal like she is. She moved to Washington so that she could march in things that she protested.

I really couldn't compare Emily to other children, but

she had friends like her who were smart. I always encouraged my children, but I never pushed any of them.

With Emily, we tried the piano and the piano didn't work. Dancing lessons didn't work. I felt sorry for her, because I studied dancing 15 years and loved it and then I studied music for eight years. And to this day, I don't do it as often as I like, because I don't have the time, but I could sit down at the piano every day, if I had the time, and play for a half hour. As I told you, it's my psychiatrist.

I don't think I pushed my sons into athletics, but they loved sports. And I think they never got into trouble simply because they were athletes. They were disciplined. Athletics teach you to be disciplined.

Emily had friends—nice kids—children I didn't have to worry about when she was in their company.

In Emily's high school days, she had a little crowd of girls. But sometimes they weren't very nice to her, because she was Jewish. She was the only Jewish girl in that crowd. I felt anti-Semitic feelings when I was growing up, but I think it was worse when my girls were growing up. I know that Emily was in this little group of girls that gathered all the time. One day, they all got mad at Emily. She shared a locker with somebody and they took everything out of her locker and laid it on the floor at school. Then they had a meeting and they wouldn't let Emily attend. I called one of the mothers up and said, "What if it was your daughter they did this to? I think you ought to talk to them." There was a ringleader, naturally. That was a very sad time in her life. It was Junior High School. It was because she was a Jewish girl and the ringleader had created the whole plot—the rest of the girls just went along with her. They excluded Emily, because she was a Jewish girl.

She cried. I consoled her, but there was nothing I could tell her, because she was so brokenhearted. You can't reason with them. It's a critical time in their life when it means something to have friends. They don't understand the hatred or exclusion and they don't even know why they're being treated that way.

As you get older, I think you get a little tougher.

I explained that's how the world works sometimes regarding Israel and being Jewish. We talked about all these things. I told her that we had to deal with things like this throughout our lives.

One thing that I remember about being Jewish and experiencing anti-Semitism is that when I got to Ohio State University, all the sororities have a pledge party on a certain day. On the first day of pledging and going to sorority houses, I remember KAPPA, KAPPA, GAMMA had sent me an invitation. My maiden name was Frank which isn't exactly a Jewish name. And they asked me to come and I went to the sorority house. In the conversation, I said that I was Jewish and they never asked me back. They never had a Jewish girl in their sorority. No, sororities were definitely Christian or Jewish. So, the Jewish Sorority asked me, it was Alpha, Phi, Epsilon. Today in fact, I'm having lunch with three former sorority sisters. We're planning a reunion back here. I'm trying to raise money for the new addition to the house at Ohio State University. Now,

25 percent of the girls there are non-Jews. It's the most outstanding sorority at Ohio State University academically and in doing community improvement. It includes everybody.

Today things have gotten better, because now all the fraternities and sororities take Jewish students. They are no longer exclusively Jewish or Christian fraternities and sororities.

When Emily got older, she went to Tulane University in New Orleans, which she loved very much. She was on the rowing team and got to travel around the United States rowing, especially up in the Northeast. She liked the school. Then she went to Lesley College in Boston. After that, she decided to do some work at Cambridge University in England. Her major was teaching drug and alcohol-addicted babies and giving their parents an education on how to take care of their babies. Sadly these mothers had burned their children's brains while in the womb. They were wards of the state and unable to get an education, because of the damage to their brains. Emily needs a cause and she felt this was a great one. She's like me in that way—pursuing worthy causes, where she can improve the situation and help the people that are involved in it.

I didn't have an empty nest until I was 66 years old. (Laugh) Someone said, "I bet you're sad." I said, "Oh no, I'm glad. I miss Emily but I'm glad I have an empty nest."

When she comes to town, we don't do anything really. She goes with me to the things that I have scheduled because I go to worthwhile things. Today I'm going to go hear two PhDs and the subject is *Education for Children* from zero to five. At Ohio State University, I have a school that has just received $13,350,000 dollars for five years to improve HEAD START. The woman I'm going to see today is a national authority on the subject, Ellen Mae Galinsky, and she's from Charleston, West Virginia.

Emily is my last child. The surprise. The shock of my life. She's been a joy to me simply because as I get older, she is more and more attentive. We were always close, but now we've gotten even closer.

We're not like girlfriends, because she smokes. I don't like smoking. I never smoked. She smokes down to the tip and that's the worst part of the cigarette. I don't know how many times we've tried to get her to stop.

What I hope for Emily and all my children and grandchildren is Happiness. Happiness. I hope they're happy. I hope they find it. My happiness, in the long run of life, the most important thing that you do is raise children. If you raise wonderful human beings, you've got it made. I feel like they're all good people. They're kind people.

I hope Emily finds someone. Whether she marries or doesn't marry, I don't care, but I hope she meets somebody that understands her. She's a beautiful, beautiful, person.

I'm proud of Emily because when she was in Washington, every Thanksgiving she would get a 1000 homeless people together and give them turkey dinners. She paid for it and thanked the volunteers by buying them beautiful aprons, which she let them keep, so they would remember that they were a part of something special and important. She's kind.

But she's tough like her daddy.

Like her daddy, clothes and makeup mean nothing to Emily. When she gets dressed up, she's gorgeous. I bought her a beige chiffon dress with black lace and she sent me a picture of her on her birthday. Oh my God, I kept saying "Emily if you always looked like this, you'd have a husband." (Laughs) But she won't dress up. I had to beg her to buy it. Her attitude is, "What you see is what you get." But what you see with Emily is real. You know what I'm saying? "Like me for what I am, not for what you want me to be."

Chapter 13

Synagogue Life & Traditions

*"Being among my people is a delight.
We Jews live among ourselves. I love it."*

— David Mamet

I was brought up as a reformed Jew.

My mom and dad were practicing Jews, but amazingly enough, how it used to be—they felt like they were Americans first and Jews second. Their parents came from Lithuania, Russia, and Bavaria—places where Jews were not treated well by the Russian Army. They wanted to be Americans first, because they came from places that treated them like second-class citizens. My mother and father became reformed Jews, not conservative or orthodox, but reformed. My father was not bar mitzvahed. He was confirmed and was more of a modern Jew.

We knew we were Jewish, because we never had a Christmas tree in the house. They let us hang our stockings until we figured out there was no Santa Claus. By then we were five years old, but we never had a Christmas tree.

I just went to Temple, but never to Synagogue. I did not

learn Hebrew, which I regret, because when I go to the conservative Temple, I can't join in with the other people when they're singing their happy songs together. I'm sorry that I don't speak Hebrew. I really am. Because everybody else there does.

When my parents didn't want us to know what they were saying around the house, they spoke Yiddish. Still they weren't so good at speaking Yiddish, even though it was their parents' language. As I became older, my Judaism became more important to me. I was confirmed when I was 15 years old and wore a white dress for my confirmation. I remember that I was taller than most boys in my class—unfortunately. (Laughs)

When I got married and had children of my own, I joined the conservative synagogue, because Alex's mother was very religious. She was orthodox and kept a kosher home. In fact, she wouldn't let me go into her kitchen, because to her I was a shiksa, a gentile, because I was brought up reformed.

Alex was not a terribly observant Jew. He wouldn't hide it ever. He was proud of being a Jew, but because he was charitable, he felt like his charity forgives him from not going to the temple or synagogue. And it does. They knew they're Jewish and they didn't deny it. My husband was proud of it, but religion didn't mean a thing to Alex. His religion was giving. His father's religion was giving. In other words, if you give, that's all you have to do, except for on the holidays, when you went to the synagogue.

Well, that was his philosophy and the way it was for Alex. Still the holidays were very important to him, the High Holy

Days. They it's a beautiful time of year. Our New Year is very festive—Yom Kipper is the most important day of the year. You are supposed to fast and not have eaten anything. You're not even supposed to have water. But I cheated, because my mother always said I could have water.

When my children grew up, they took some of the traditions and brought up their children as conservatives.

I observe all the holidays today and they mean a lot to me. For Yom Kipper, you ask forgiveness for the sins you have committed against anybody. I think the prayers you say so many times makes you say to yourself, "When will we stop singing this prayer?" You're supposed to be in the Synagogue all day. You start at night at sundown, and very orthodox Jews like my mother-in-law, they won't even use a light switch. They turn the lights on before the holidays and they don't turn them off until holidays are over, because they aren't supposed to touch the light switch.

I feel transformed on those days. It's like a cleansing. You start anew and you have a wonderful feeling.

For Rosh Hashanah, that's a happy holiday and it starts the New Year. We read the Torah the whole time and then when the Torah starts again, it's New Year's Day. It comes at different times and is never on the same day ever and goes according to the Jewish calendar.

Passover is the happiest holiday of them all, because it celebrates when the Jews left Egypt and set up housekeeping in a new area after traveling through the Red Sea.

Moses spoke to God and God gave him the Ten Commandments. If we lived by the Ten Commandments, this would be a beautiful world. And I definitely believe that. Wasn't that wise? It's basic stuff.

David was a wonderful character. The Psalms are beautiful. If you read the Psalms at various times of your life, the Psalms will fit into your life to help you in whatever you're doing.

I greatly admired Golda Meir. She said something that to this day can be said and it can be said in the future. "Until the Muslim women love their children more than they hate Israel, there will never be peace." Think about that. They send their children to go off and bomb other people. They don't object. They feel like they're saints. She was a very wise woman and in her time was a super-hero—a female Prime Minister. She lived in the United States, you know, in Minnesota.

Chanukah was a happy holiday, because we got a present every day. Not much of a present, but it was wrapped up and we got a present every day for eight days. Chanukah came from when they were defending the temple at Masada. They took the containers that held the oil for our candles and they dumped them over. And we had to have the oil for our eternal light, which should never go out. Well, when they dumped all the oil out, there was just one container of oil left and it was supposed to last for just a couple of days, but it lasted for eight days until they could get oil. So we celebrate that holiday, because it's a big deal in history and because Christmas is so close to Chanukah, we celebrate it—to give our children a celebration.

I feel the commercialization of Christmas has caused many people to miss the true reason and meaning behind the season. It becomes a money holiday and people start in September with their decorations, presents, and everything. Then in one day, the whole thing is over. Morning, it's Christmas and at night, Christmas is over.

We're celebrating Passover this weekend at my daughter's home. Joann is complaining a little bit about the difficulty of preparing a big dinner and she's going to be 60 on her next birthday. Remember I had a child at home until I was 66. So I had Passover at my house from the age of 24 until the age of 66 years old. I always made the Passover meal.

The Passover meal is eight or nine courses, maybe a ten-course meal, and everything we eat is a reminder of when the Jews fled Egyptian bondage. They were slaves in Egypt where they built the pyramids. How they built them without the modern technology of lifting is simply amazing. It was male labor that lifted it, that of Jewish slaves who built the pyramids.

Passover is about tradition. Tradition. That was a miracle, truly a miracle, when God caused the plagues, one after another until the head of the Egyptian government said, "They can go." He let them go and when they got to the Red Sea, a miracle was delivered. The Red Sea, now according to modern day, they think it might have been a tsunami that came at a very critical time. But we don't know, because we didn't have modern science, but it happened. It happened. Because as I read the Bible, they don't cover up things that aren't nice. When they say he begat, begat, begat, well it's not nice to begat, but it was in the Bible. It was just like it happened.

Let me tell you about the Bible, the Old Testament has all the bad things mixed in with the good things. They begat,

begat, they told it all in there. You know? And God punished people then when they did the wrong thing. And HE saved their lives when they did the good things. And when the Red Sea opened up—I'm not sure that the sea opened up—I think they had a tsunami and that wave came in and wiped those men out in that moment. It was a miracle that happened. And of course, the Jewish people were free. The fact is that the Bible was written at the time while all these things were happening.

Now I don't want to cast aspersions on anybody, but from what I know, the Christian Bible was not written until 200 years after the death of Christ. And why wasn't it? Why? The only people who knew how to write in the Roman language (Latin) were the Jews, the scribes. They were the scribes. And they wrote history. And now the Romans weren't going to preach Jesus, because they didn't like Jesus. So they never mentioned him. And they just told things that the Romans did. Therefore, did you ever sit in a circle and say a sentence in the beginning and by the time it gets to the last person, you wonder if the first statement and the last one are even related. So you cannot exactly say then what happened, and if what is in the Bible really happened.

We'll know in the end, won't we?

Now the saints glorified him and most of them were Jewish originally and they were hyping up Jesus. He was a great man. Absolutely a great man, but I'm not sure he wanted to start another religion, because he was training to be a Rabbi.

All Jewish people in some way or another celebrate Passover. It has always been important to my family. Even today, this Passover morning 2016, it's still very important to me.

At sundown, I'm doing what my forefathers did for thousands of years. For this year's Passover I'm not doing anything but the Charoset with chopped walnuts and apples, to remind us of the mortar that the slaves used to build the pyramids. I'm going to chop and prep. And we will have the Seder at my daughter's home in Oldsmar.

For this huge meal everything is flourless. We don't use flour. We use Matzo meal. We don't use flour, because as the Jews were fleeing, they didn't have time for their bread to be done. We don't eat anything with flour in it for a week. It's to remind us of our tradition. Everything is there to remind us of our tradition. We eat horseradish to remind us of how bitter their lives were. Everything we eat that night is to remind us of our tradition. Gefilte fish, matzo ball soup, brisket traditionally, a dish called tzimmes, which is sweet potatoes, white potatoes, prunes, carrots, and sometimes oranges, all baked together—it's delicious.

It's a big job to get the dishes out. That's why I offered to have it at a restaurant this year. I told her that I can't have it at home anymore. I can't do it. I just want to say that I believe in tradition very strongly.

To me, the Passover holiday means continuity—the continuity of Judaism—from one generation to the next. Hopefully we can pass this on to our grandchildren and great-grandchildren. Hopefully. I'm doing my best to instill it. All the intermarriage in our family converted. My daughter-in-law, who converted, became the head of the whole Jewish Federation of

Tampa Bay for four years, where she raised millions of dollars for them. She was a convert and the president of Beth Shalom in Sarasota. So I'm all for conversions. And my grandson—his wife converted, too. He insisted on her being Jewish and she's Lebanese. If we don't have conversions, the traditions and Judaism will fade away and be gone. We're 0.2 percent of the world's population. It's a drop in the bucket. Miniscule. And little Israel survived. Isn't that amazing? The Greek Empire, the Roman Empire, and Spain kicked us out in 1492.

I'm proud of being Jewish. When you read the history of the Jews and see all the empires that have fallen and you see all these things happening and the Jews have held out all these Arab countries for thousands of years. We've been here thousands of years and we're still here with all odds against us. Every Arab nation has been against Israel.

I feel that while the hand of God is with Israel, I think he's angry at the world right now, because we're having these terrible weather conditions with horrible winters and summers. I think he's telling the world something. "You are going away from religion. Going away from God. And because of that, your morals have dropped. Your standards have dropped." We are no longer guided by right and wrong. I definitely believe there is a right and wrong way to do things.

For Passover, the Bible is our prayer. We talk about the whole book of Exodus. We have a book with all the services in it. Now that we have great-grandchildren, it's not much of a service. We're chasing them around the house. (Laughs) But we try and it still feels like Passover.

I sometimes have some regrets for not being as religious

as I could have been. The reason for that is the first generation of Jews was born in the United States and the US was so different from Europe, in that they wanted to be Americans first and Jews second. My parents joined the Reform movement, and the reform movement takes a lot of tradition away from Judaism. My husband was raised in the Orthodox religion, which is stuffed with tradition, tradition, tradition, and of course, he wasn't that religious, so it didn't bother him. But when I would go to his Synagogue, I couldn't even read one word of Hebrew and everybody in the congregation reads Hebrew. They took it as children and learned to read Hebrew. I didn't have any of that. My grandmother who was the daughter of rabbi was taught Hebrew and women were not taught Hebrew in Europe. Only the men learned Hebrew and went to the prayer sessions and read out of the Torah. Women did not. And now the reform religion has gotten much more traditional, because they feel that it's tradition that helps keep you religious.

So I can't regret it, because my parents did what they thought was best for their children by becoming Americans.

Regarding advice to my family and their Judaism?

Most of my family are conservative Jews. Most of the laws that we have in Judaism—for instance, not eating shellfish and all that—were made because we did not have refrigeration. When you kill a pig on one day and the temperature never goes under 100 degrees for 24 hours, that pig has maggots in and you shouldn't eat it. The same is true of shrimp. So they did away with a lot of the dietary laws, simply because they realized why they made those laws. The conservatives keep a lot of them. I'm a conservative Jew, but I'm not truly conservative, because I was raised reformed.

I'm interested in the survival of every one of the charities I'm involved with and that's why I do that. Yet they are not all equally important. I mean I love the arts, I studied dancing and piano, but what takes prime focus is my commitment to education and Judaism.

Chapter 14

Charity Begins at Home

> "Where there is charity and wisdom,
> there is neither fear nor ignorance."
>
> — Francis of Assisi

Early influences in my life set me up to be the giving person I became later in life and to feel for other people.

We lived in neighborhood where the plant was located and most of the people who lived there were quite poor. We had a little more money than our neighbors, but not a lot more. It probably seemed like more money, because we owned our house and most of the rest of the people rented.

Until I was ten years old, I was brought up in that milieu. I remember my mother cooking on holidays for a lot of other people.

I inherited a lot of this from my parents—this ability to feel for and have empathy for people. It runs in our family. I have a little granddaughter who is so empathetic with people, that when she sees kids coming with the same dress every day, she takes a bag of clothes and gives it to them, clothes that her mom was ready to give away—shoes and everything.

Then she would beg her mother to give away some of her nice clothes for the little child. She would always bring extra food for her in school. She has this giving spirit already.

Regarding philanthropy and a need to act, there are a lot of people who have it—this ability to give. They really do. There's a lot of wonderful giving in this community of Sarasota. Did you know that Sarasota County is the most giving county per capita in the United States? I say that, "Sarasota County is the county with the heart on it."

The restaurant business gave us the means to go and give. My husband was very giving. Not only was he giving but he would also go out and get involved and raise money. In fact, he raised 31-and-half million dollars for the Salvation Army over a five-year period.

My husband was not religious, but he respected what you believed in and he wanted you to respect what he believed in. He didn't want you to try to change him.

As it turns out, the Salvation Army didn't have a pension plan. They took out for uniforms, car, housing, and for food from their pay. They didn't have much social security. So when Alex got down here, they were all living in mobile homes. He said, "Why are you living in mobile homes?"

"Well," they said, "they don't pay a lot at Salvation Army, because they're not allowed to raise money for our salaries. They can only raise money for their programs." Alex thought it was awful. So he got involved. He spoke to the people in the South East Division of the Salvation Army in Atlanta, Georgia. He found that they needed 25 million dollars for the pension plan for the southeast end of the territory. Alex told the powers that be, "You give me five years and a paid professional and I will have your money."

Five years later, he had raised 31 *million* dollars! $25,000,000 million dollars for a pension plan; $5,000,000 million dollars for a new chapel in Atlanta; and $1,000,000 dollars for a dorm to train women officers.

At times when he was challenged and people would say, "Why would a Jewish man raise that kind of money for the Salvation Army, a Christian organization?"

Alex always had an answer. And his answer was in granite on the grounds of the Salvation Army on 10th street. "We are all descended from Abraham, Isaac, and Jacob. We are all brothers with every human in the world. And when my brothers are in need, when he has nowhere else to turn, he can turn to the Salvation Army."

It's so true. They're the best-run organization in the United States—only 9% goes to their administration—the rest goes to charity.

He was involved with the Salvation Army over the course of his life. It's something that I gladly and proudly continued after his death. In fact, I just spoke to a captain of the Salvation Army on the phone.

When I hear those bells ringing, I think they're wonderful. They're wonderful people. I helped ring bells one year. I did this at Publix on Longboat Key. I had fun, because I knew all the people going in there. And if they didn't give me enough money, I'd say, "Cheapskate." (Laughs)

Our philanthropy was something that we developed together. We were both givers. I don't think we realized it until we got married and got some money that we believed so much in sharing. We didn't talk about it. It was just a natural thing. What he liked he liked. What I liked, I liked.

Alex loved the Boys and Girls clubs, because they helped children. In 1978, the Boys Club had 90 boys—it was confined to just boys then—and they were about to go under, because they didn't have enough money to pay salaries for the next three months and they couldn't get any more money until next year. So Alex got involved and got three men including himself to each give $25,000 to save the Boys and Girls Club. And now they have 4200 members in the Sarasota, Bradenton, and Venice Boys and Girls Club.

One of the charities that is the nearest and dearest to my heart is All Faiths Food Bank. It is so important, because if young people are hungry, they can't learn in school. We are going to have a whole generation, since one out of every five children don't have enough to eat. That means we are going to have to build more penitentiaries, because those children can't learn. You can't be hungry and sit in school and your brain doesn't work. You got to feed it.

I have great respect and admiration for the Jewish Family and Children Services. They are without a doubt, the most amazing organization. 90 percent of the money is raised by Jewish people. Twenty percent of the money is used to help elderly Jewish people and their needs. The other 80 percent goes to help non-Jews. That's the God's truth. They're looking out for veterans, people who have been in jail, and for families who can't make it, and who have problem with the rent and need food. It's a beautiful organization.

Glasser-Schoenbaum is one of Alex's favorites and mine, too. We serve about 12,000 people a month. We service people from ages zero to 100. It helps with housing: the blind; the disabled; the hungry, and the homeless. If you can pay something, we ask that you pay something, but if you have no money and can't, you're not kicked out.

We were very active with charities back in West Virginia. We had five Shoney's in the Charleston area, so we were involved in a lot of giving. I feel that the duty of a person who has the means is to share. Absolutely share. You put away enough so that you can live the rest of your life, and you give the rest away. And you give it while you live, because if you give it when you die, you don't know what they're going to do with your money.

I mean you may leave it to your church for a program on Christmas and then the roof is leaking. Well then, when they need money, your money will go for that, and there will be no more Christmas party or program. You give it while you live, so you can have the joy of seeing what your money does.

My life was full of activities pertaining to what the children were doing, like being a den mother and Cub Scout leader. I was also very active in the sisterhood of the local temples, in Hadassah which is an international organization, and the National Council of Jewish Women.

When I left Charleston I was up to being president of Hadassah. They're all causes and organizations that I believed in and was involved with. It wasn't just being a mother. I got involved. And in my life now, I'm involved in everything. I want others to know that I have been involved in helping people and it started when I was young.

Here is a story from when we were just starting out. Someone came to my husband and asked him for some money. We were married in April and he was making $40 a week selling cars. This individual came to us in September for a gift. We were living in a $40 a month furnished apartment. So $40 dollars or one week's pay would go for our rent. They came to Alex and he gave them a $100, which is pretty dear, because it was over two-week's salary. So when it came to January when he had to pay it, Alex didn't have it. So we skimped on our budget to give them that $100.00.

My husband was always very charitable, even when we didn't have the money. And we always paid it off. Of course in two years, he was able to make pledges and pay them off right away. I really loved and respected that the most about Alex. He could have been my grandmother's child, simply because he just loved to give. He loved to give.

The difference between my husband and me is that with Alex, you had to come back and beg him for it. If your cause touches my heart, I give right away. I have to believe in it. I find that most of my giving goes to education, underprivileged people, and building an organization that really could do a lot of good in the world.

Alex loved to give. Grandma's giving was for Israel. And today, whenever I do something for Israel, I feel like I'm carrying out what my grandmother started. She was a beautiful woman. Small in stature, but a heart as big as the world. You got to remember when my grandmother was saving that money, there was no radio, no television—it was just the love of Israel. It was not Israel at that time. It was Palestine.

Grandma taught me, but I didn't realize it at the time. My grandmother planted those roots, because it's something that happens inside of you from exposure. I didn't say, "Look at what my grandmother is teaching me," it just happened.

So the seeds of giving were planted by Grandma, and then when I met Alex, he was so much like her in that he was so giving. But he was tough—I mean not with me, never with me. But he had to be tough to get to where he got. He was a Leo on top and a lamb on the bottom. Actually he was a pussycat.

When I was raising our two boys, we lived in a one-bedroom apartment, but we built a house shortly after that. When the boys were two and three, we moved into a new home. When I got pregnant, we had just moved to Charleston. We lived with Alex's mother since her three other sons were in the service. My father-in-law was not well and was in a sanitarium out in California, so we moved in with her and I didn't want to get pregnant until I had a home of my own.

I was involved mainly in my children's lives and all the religious organizations in my late twenties.

We became middle-class citizens. I gave my children a wonderful childhood like the one I had. I used to take lunch over to the high school, because the band played at noon and my children would eat lunch over there. I exposed my children to a lot of neat stuff. We lived a block from the high school. I brought them sandwiches. Healthy foods. We didn't have Twinkies. They were little kids, two and three years old and were not in school yet. The band was practicing. They were active boys and would sit down and eat lunch that way and watch the band.

They had a lot of freedom back then. They'd play out in the yard and not have to come home until dark. You didn't have to worry about somebody picking them up and molesting them. It was just a different world, a different world. The best, the best, the best.

At this time, Alex is working a lot and he's building a big business—a legacy and I was building mine, too. Alex wasn't home a lot, so I did most of the parenting, which was fine with me. He was doing it for us, so why would I object? Whatever it was, we did it.

When I got some time and the children were in school, I was able to get involved and be useful to the community such as in the Jewish community. We had nice-size Jewish community in Charleston, but not as large as Sarasota's Jewish community, but I would say there were at least 300 families. We joined Temple Beth Israel first. They didn't do Bar or Bat mitzvah and Alex's mother was Orthodox and they believed in Bar and Bat mitzvah. I was brought up reformed and we were confirmed. Because of that, we joined the conservative Synagogue.

I got involved with Jewish groups, like B'nai Jacob's auxiliary, the women's division, that's what I called it. I also belonged to my reformed temple, because my husband really didn't care if we were conservative or reformed—we just had to be Jewish. And I kept my membership with the Reformed Temple, which we joined when we got Charleston. The Synagogue at that time was a miserable looking place and I never even walked into it. It was old and in a bad section of town. Now they have a beautiful one.

At this time, I was involved doing bake sales. With my husband being in the business, we even did bake sales in school for the children. I got involved in anything that involved my children. The School. The Synagogue. Whatever they were involved in. You have to want to make their life better. You do it for your child. For all the children.

Because my husband was in the restaurant business, Shoney's has already started and my youngest child was a year old, they thought we could defray expenses. We gave them plates, napkins, and forks. We became like a supply house. When they needed something I'd say, "Call my husband up." I delegated.

Back then I started getting involved and filling my schedule and appointment book. I guess you can attribute that as to the reason why I am that way today. Am I the same person? I guess, but I'm grown up now. And instead of giving paper plates away, I give away millions of dollars. (Laughs)

I didn't start sitting on boards and really give big gifts away until my husband passed away, because up until that time, any big philanthropic gifts were given by Alex.

Remember, I had a child at home until I was 66, when I became an empty nester. When Emily left for college and the University of Tulane in 1966, I wasn't twiddling my thumbs. I was too busy. I had an exercise class and I played Mahjong. I went out with my friends for lunch and went to meetings like Hadassah, National Council for Jewish Women, and PTA meetings.

I got involved with these organizations because there was a need for money. I contributed and I believed in their causes. In fact, Hadassah has a hospital and one day, we will see a cure for cancer coming out of that hospital. The research that they are doing is fabulous. Yes, I think that it is possible to cure cancer and I think they will find it. I think that someday they will find it, because now our information highway is getting so full. They're going to find it.

While I give easily, I not only look at the greater good, but I look the charity up in Charity Navigator. It's a book that ranks charities from the returns sent in to the IRS and it's a trusted rating service that ranks all the nonprofits in the United States.

There are some charities that give maybe 10 percent of their donations to the cause and the rest goes to expenses. I do my research, because I want the money to get to where it needs to go to help people. It's just intelligent to do your research.

I vet the charities and believe they are responsible for making sure the funds go to whoever it can help the most—to the people that they promised to do it for.

If you want to give money, give to All Faiths Food Bank and you'll know where the money goes, because they are a tightly run ship.

Hadassah, as you may know started out as nursing group that traveled to Israel before Israel became a country. At that time, there were no pipes and plumbing throughout the country. Everyone was going to the bathroom in ditches. There was no sanitation in Palestine. These nurses went over there because they had a lot of problems with people's health. They became a group and formed a hospital—Hadassah Hospital.

There is a story about that hospital during the Six Day War—an interesting time of Israel's life. During this war, they were attacked on our holiest day of all, Yom Kipper, because everyone was in Temple and not home. They attacked the temples and told all the Arabs in Palestine, "Leave! Leave! We're going to conquer this country and you can have your homes back and everything." Well, 930,000 Arabs left Israel and we won the war. In fact, Hadassah Hospital was absolutely snowed in. There were volunteer doctors coming up a road on a bus and they bombed them from above. They left the bombs from that bombing of the bus there for years to remind people what happened when these volunteers were going up to help. And they were not only helping the Jewish people, but they were helping the Palestinians who came to the hospital.

I have had a strong commitment with this organization. When I got to Charleston in 1943, I was 25 years old and it was before I had children, so I joined immediately.

I am still involved today and go to meetings here in Sarasota. When I left Charleston, I was going to be the President of Hadassah's board. It's one of the organizations at the top of my list. Let me tell you about the hospital. If you're Muslim, you can go there and get help. If you're Christian, you can go there and get help. If you're Jewish, you can go there and get help. They don't care what creed you are, they just want to help. They don't care about race or creed.

That's the way the world should be and the way the

Salvation Army is, no matter what race, color, or creed. Yes that's why it was Alex's passion and mine, too.

Every time I hear that bell ring, it touches my heart and I feel something for these people and that's because it's the best run organization in the world dollar-wise, the Salvation Army.

Amazingly, I didn't do too much, because my husband was giving to all the things that I'm giving to now. He was the one who gave. He never objected to anything I spent or wanted to give to. He was wonderful about that. When it came to giving I would and could give to anything I wanted to give to. Still, when it came to giving, he did the big giving. He was not in control. If I said I wanted to give $5000 to Hadassah, he would never deny me.

The major philanthropy and the passing of the giving torch, so to speak, was given to me after he passed away.

It's something I take very seriously and something that is so important to me. Giving. But when you give, you have to be careful. As Ronald Reagan said, "Trust and verify." It's not a handshake anymore. My husband was a handshake guy. His handshake was his word. But when people didn't treat him that way, like if you told him that you were going to call him up at noon and you called after noon, he would give you hell. Your word is your honor. Especially when it comes to giving.

Part Three

SETTLING DOWN IN THE SUNSHINE STATE

Chapter 15

On the Move: Florida

"We keep moving forward, opening new doors, and doing new things, because we're curious and curiosity keeps leading us down new paths."

— Walt Disney

The time had come. That sweet time. When the couple could kick back and relax a little bit. A time when Betty's Big Boy didn't have to do all the heavy lifting that he did in the early days. There were still business trips and Alex was still working, but the pace had changed. And while Betty still had nine-year-old Emily at home, life was a little simpler for the Schoenbaums. It was the three of them at home now. The three older children were already carving out the dreams of what their lives would become. For Alex, Betty, and Emily, the southern breezes and sunshine of the sunshine state called to them, enticed them, and invited them to stay a while.

It was around 1975 and Alex got to the point in life where he wanted a respite and time off.

We came down a year before and looked around the east coast of Florida. We'd been there several times before and we'd also been to Sarasota, because Alex's family used to come down here to vacation. There was a big development on Mound Street where the Boston Red Sox used to stay between Osprey and 301. Alex's family rented a unit when they would come down for three months. This was back when Ted Williams was playing for the Red Sox. It was also a time, 1950, when they were filming *The Greatest Show on Earth*. I remember it so well, especially when they filmed that scene going down Main Street after the train wreck. My husband was there with our boys. At the time, they were three and four years old and Alex had the three-year-old, Jeffry, on his shoulder. In the movie, you can barely see that it is Alex Schoenbaum or our son, but there they were in *The Greatest Show on Earth*. You can't really tell that it's Alex, but we know that it is.

That's really the first time we encountered Sarasota. There was one thing on St. Armand's Circle, the Columbia Restaurant. I even remember that the handles that opened the beautiful doors were brass fish. We would take the road and go out to Longboat Key, which back then was not much of a road.

On the left side, there would be fishing shacks and on the right, there would be dilapidated homes until you got out to the Field Club. There was one hotel owned by a Frenchman, near where the Publix is today. I remember the tide would come over under the hotel. When we were vacationing back then with Alex's family, the big place was

Lido Beach. Siesta was not as popular then. There were only 12,500 people here in Sarasota in 1950.

When we were trying to figure where we wanted to stay in Florida, we started in Vero Beach and went all the way down the coast. I didn't want to live on the east coast at all. Highway I-95 goes from Maine to Key West and they were all easterners. They are a little aggressive for me and I didn't want to raise my daughter in that milieu. So we went around the coast and through Naples. I loved Naples, but there was not a Jewish Temple there, so we came up to Fort Myers. The problem there was that the beach was so far from the town, and I didn't want to live on the beach and have to travel into town. So we came up to Sarasota. The more we looked around, the more we decided it would be Sarasota. Perhaps it was because we knew the town already. We rented a home on Longboat Key for a year, which gave us some time to figure where we wanted to live. At this time, we had our nine-year-old daughter, Emily, with us. She had to go to school, so when we moved there, we took it for a year. I soon found out there was no school bus on Longboat and that I would have to go from the 2800 block on Gulf of Mexico Drive all the way to Bird Key so she could be picked up by a school bus.

I was 57 years old. I had the responsibility every day to wait for and pick up Emily at 3 p.m. We decided that we didn't want to raise her in a neighborhood with no children. That contributed to our decision to rent a condo at Tortuga on Siesta Key. There were a lot of homes and developments where families lived, so she would be able play with children. We had a big gorgeous condominium with a 100-foot-long front porch and we lived there for ten years until she went away to college.

Then we built a place on Longboat Key at 5541 Gulf of Mexico Drive, across from *Euphemia Haye*. My husband wanted to build a home and I told him, "Alex, you still travel with the business and I don't want to be left in the house all by myself on the beach." I'd rather have something built where I have neighbors in the building. Because of flood zone restrictions, on the first floor, we built a 12-car garage. We also built four apartments. The front apartments had three bedrooms and two baths that overlooked the Gulf and the back apartments had two bedrooms and two baths that overlooked the bay. We rented those out and I had a 5600 square foot home built on the top, a two-story home, with two-story window bedroom suites, a living room suite, an office suite, and the kitchen. I had an elevator that came up in the middle and in the back was my guest suite for our children. I had a great room with lots of sofa beds, two bedrooms, a kitchen, and laundry room. They never did find the kitchen. (Laughs) I don't think the stove was ever used, because they would come up to my apartment and visit. But it was ideal, because when Alex and I wanted to go to sleep, the kids wanted to play, so we put them in the back. We were there for eleven years. You have to check out the building that I built there. It's beautiful.

The main reason I moved off the Key to downtown, was because while I was still driving, I was followed three times and put in very precarious situations. I decided I'm not going to get out of the Van Wezel at 10 o'clock at night and drive by myself to Longboat Key. Once when I was followed home, they stopped near the light over the first bridge. It's a straight drag there. There was an SUV with tinted windows. I was going about 40 mph and he was waiting for me. He came at me at about, I swear, 80 mph and I thought he was going to crash into me. I was driving down Longboat Key about 80-90 mph with no place to stop, until you get to Buttonwood Harbor and they didn't have the store open then. Near my house, there was a convenience store and they called the police but they were never caught.

There was another time when a car followed me right into my garage. I went to the convenience store again and called the police and they were never caught, but the people from the convenience store helped me go back to my apartment.

Then the last time, I pulled into my garage, four men were sitting in my parking space smoking in my garage. Of course, I left right away. This time the convenience store was closed, so I drove to the fire station. They were all sleeping. I woke them up and they got me home. I just said, "This is ridiculous." I was scared and worried and thought that one of these days, they're going to catch me and do something.

That was the impetus for my move downtown. I looked around and Sarabande was being built at the time. Alex had passed away in 1996. I was 79. I was mobile and I just had this balance problem.

I want to tell you that Alex could never live this high up in the air. The fourth floor would be as high as he would go, because he didn't like heights. I love my view here. There is not a better view of Sarasota than in my condo. You can see Siesta Key over there, you can see the interstate from the back, and the only thing you can't see is Selby Gardens. I have four balconies and I can see everything. My views are fantastic and before they built that new building, I could see the Sunshine Skyway Bridge.

Living downtown is fabulous. You're close to the Opera House, Florida Studio Theatre, Asolo, and the Van Wezel. Everything is within your reach and there are a lot of restaurants to go to and events downtown. It's just very convenient.

Downtown is the favorite place I've lived, but with what they are doing with it, it's not going to be my favorite. I want to know what is wrong with the city commissioners giving permits for these people to build over to the curb. They put these mammoth things sitting right on the curb. What's wrong with the city commissioners? It's deplorable.

Maybe I'll have to run for mayor on my 100th birthday.

What would I do if I had a magic wand—I'd make sure every building has to have at least an eight-foot setback for sidewalks and put some green around it. This is beginning to look like Miami with condos and hotels.

I do love the Ringling Bridge. It's wonderful. Gil Waters is an angel, the way he stood up for that bridge. To look at the bridge from my home—it's a thrill.

Chapter 16

World Traveler

"The real voyage of discovery consists not in seeking new landscapes, but in having new eyes."

— Marcel Proust

I've traveled a lot.

At first I traveled a lot, because when Alex opened a new store, if I was able to have someone look after the children, I would accompany him.

My favorite place I've traveled to on earth—Israel—is a democracy that is now approaching its 70th birthday. It was once a barren desert when the Jews took it over. The only living beings in that desert were Bedouin Arabs, who lived in tents and grazed their goats. We worried about the children who were born to those Arabs, so we sent teachers around to the tents to teach the children how to read.

Israel is a total democracy and the only one in the Middle East. It's truly a miracle, because they truly don't have a lot of water—every drop of water is recycled. What comes out of the toilet is recycled and goes into the fields.

Politically, if there are two people left in Israel, they could and would argue. But you're going to have that in any country. When people don't agree with what the head of the government is doing, they are no different than any other countries. Yet the technology that comes out of Israel is amazing. I don't know how many Nobel prizes have come out of Israel compared to how few have been produced by Muslim countries.

People have to understand that Israel was there before the Muslims ever came to the land in the Fourth Century. The Jews lived in Palestine. There were Jews and Christians there, but there were not Muslims. In fact, Muhammad had never been to Jerusalem, and Jerusalem was never mentioned in the Koran.

Israel is my favorite place, because Jews can go there and be a part of a country where they're safe. Yet I'm worried by the way they are being besieged by all the countries all around them. They're having a hard time. You can go down the street in Israel and be stabbed by a Muslim. I worry about that, because people can't go out.

Another favorite place I've traveled is Italy. I truly loved Italy. All of it. I went there after the war and they are such friendly and happy people. The food is great. The scenery is great and I loved the whole feeling.

Having traveled to France, I found that they weren't too friendly to Americans. They forget about Omaha Beach.

Another place I love is Buenos Aires. I loved the dancing and the people are very educated, proud, and elegant.

I love Asia as well. I have been to China three times and twice to Japan. In fact, we had a Big Boy Restaurant in Japan. As far as China is concerned, it's unfathomable. You wonder how it exists and how they control their country with so many people in it. I walked on the Great Wall. I liked Japan better than China. The people are more educated in Japan than in China.

We went to all the temples. I've also been to Thailand, South America, Spain, Brussels, England, Germany, and all the Scandinavian countries when we went with the symphony from Sarasota.

I've been to Russia twice. The first time I went, it was tough. I remembered that people didn't smile then. You would walk down the street and they had scaffolding over the roof because of the poor construction and parts of the building would fall from the buildings over the sidewalk and hit people. This is when it was communistic. The people were not happy and didn't understand a word of English. We were watched while we were there the first time. Someone was always on the bus that we were on that we recognized, so we knew we were being tailed. I wasn't afraid, because I hadn't done anything wrong and I was with a group.

The place that surprised me the most was when I was in Africa—the northern part, Morocco. I was surprised that it was nicer than I thought it would be.

Still I think the place that shocked me most was my first visit to Israel—that they had taken this land and grew a forest. They put a little twig in and the only place they have a hole is where they plant the tree and when they turn the hoses on, it only waters that root. That's how they grew those forests. Amazingly bright people. Now if they could only desalinate water to the extent that they could afford it, wouldn't that be wonderful?

The Joy of Giving is the Joy of Living

In the United States, to be honest with you, I think that one of the most beautiful resorts in all the world is the Greenbriar Hotel in Lewisburg, West Virginia. It's truly southern hospitality in a beautiful environment. Outside you see some 3000 mum plants in various parts of the grounds. Also on the grounds, they have beautiful homes where US presidents would vacation as a getaway from Washington DC.

During the Second World War, under a mountain right on the grounds of the Greenbriar, they had a facility set up where congress could meet in the event that war ever got to the United States. In West Virginia, we don't have big mountains—we have low mountains. Therefore, they are heavily forested with almost every kind of wood and tree that can be grown in this hemisphere. It's just a beautiful, lovely, and charming place that's very well kept with three golf courses, lots of tennis courts, swimming areas, and a bowling alley.

Places I'd still like to go?

I'd like to go on a safari and I would love to go see the Taj Mahal in India. We did visit India on a cruise, but it was a small town. I would have liked to have traveled to Australia, but it's so far on the plane. I've been to a lot of countries though. I have even been to Alaska in the summer time when it wasn't so cold. Beautiful scenery and the icebergs are awesome—it's just an enchanting place.

I've also been to Hawaii, but once you go there, you really don't want to go back, because we have beautiful weather and beaches right here in Sarasota.

Why would I go there, when I already live in Paradise?

Chapter 17

Empty Nest

"There are only two lasting bequests we can hope to give our children. One of these is roots, the other, wings."

— Johann Wolfgang von Goethe

After Emily went away to college, for the first time in my life at 66 years old, I had no responsibility except to get dinner on the table. It's not that I didn't have any place to go.

I had an empty nest.

Most experience that time as an empty nest much earlier. They are married in their twenties, have children in their thirties, and by their fifties, they have an empty nest. For me it didn't happen until I was 66. So my life was different. I had an empty nest as I entered old age. (Laughs).

I didn't plan it. I didn't decide it, honey. It just came. (Laughs) My kids just came. No, the last one did. In fact, I told you that Emily's middle initial was a B, because her grandfather was "Emil B." as in Boris Schoenbaum. He died not long before she was born. Usually Jewish people are named after somebody who has died. So I called her Emily B. for Boris Schoenbaum. But the B also stood for "Boo

Boo," which I didn't tell her until she grew up. (Laughs) Well, she knew that for me at age 48½ years old, she was a "Boo Boo." But the nicest "Boo Boo" I ever had, a wonderful "Boo Boo."

In an empty nest, that's when I really came into my own.

I was a homemaker. I was never a housewife. I did the cooking. Nobody else ever did the cooking. A housewife is the one who does the housework, but I always had somebody to help, even if she only came one or two days a week to clean my house. But I was a dummy—I still used to dust it every day. Did you ever hear of a woman who dusted her house every day? I just felt that was what you were supposed to do, if you didn't do the other tasks. (Laughs)

After all, four kids are out of the house, so that's when I soared into another arena. I was always active in all the clubs. Any help they needed, I always volunteered, but I never was the head of any of these clubs, because I valued my freedom.

While I was active in many and I took chairmanships and everything else, but I was never an officer. I think more or less it was because Alex was still traveling and opening up stores, so quite often I would go with him for the opening, if it was a nice-sized town.

Once we went on a tour of all the Shoney's in the Deep South. I'm talking about Louisiana, Alabama, Georgia, North and South Carolina, and Florida. We visited all of them—every town that had even a small Shoney's, we went there and they would bring out the high school band. They'd march down the street and we'd be in a limousine. We were like royalty at that time. (Laughs)

Empty Nest

It was fun and it wasn't tiring, because Shoney's sometimes was the first restaurant built in those towns. In essence, Shoney's put those towns on the map.

We were treated like royalty with a parade and the mayor would come out and hand us a key to the city. Oh, we had wonderful welcomes. The town that gave us the biggest "Hurrah" was New Orleans. When I arrived at the airport and got off the plane, there was always somebody there with a bouquet of flowers and a limousine to escort us to the hotel, which was in the city. As I rode in that limousine, I kept saying, "Oh my Gosh, I'm in this limousine and they can see the flowers and everything." I thought people will think, "This must be somebody important." So I was embarrassed, because I'm not important. So I put dark glasses on and then I looked like somebody that they might recognize. (Laughs) We did have a great welcome and met many wonderful people.

I felt their warmth and their need. They were really happy and they truly appreciated us being there. Every place we went, they gave us a warm welcome.

I was free to travel on these trips with my new empty nester status.

I never said, "What do I do now?" after the nest was empty, because I never knew what I would do next. I just knew that I would be more active than just being a committee member. I became much more involved.

First of all, we had a lot of affairs at my house. In fact, we even had an affair shortly after Emily was born. At that time, I had promised the Hadassah organization to have their big fundraiser at my home. For the event, I would be either nine months pregnant at the time or have a newborn baby. Rather than get out of it, I thought, well, I will debut my child at the tea. (Laughs) So we had a big debut. There was a picture in the newspaper about how I gave a tea with my six-weeks-old child. People thought it was wonderful.

They asked. "How did I do all that?" Honey, I'm young still. At that time, I was just 49. You really start living between the ages of 40 and 50. That's a great time of your life. It really is. You have energy, if you're positive. If you're negative, you have no energy. I'm very positive and it's all based on attitude. Attitude plays a big part in the dynamic. It's the most important thing in your life. Attitude. If you say, "I hope I make it to 100," but you shouldn't say that. I do that once in a while, but I catch myself. You should say, "I know I'm going to make it to 100." It's positivity. Being positive.

It's a beautiful day, not it's partly cloudy. But when I do see cloudy weather lately, I say, "Oh thank God, we need rain so badly."

It's how you look at things. I think one of the things that I do, that a lot of people don't do, is I notice certain things—like trees, for example. As I drive, I watch them and see them after it rains, how their leaves glisten and how when it doesn't rain, they get dull and yellowish.

My father taught me to adore nature. When we used to live out at the cottage, he'd plant vegetables. Daddy had a vegetable garden, a herb garden—all kinds of gardens. I think he taught me to appreciate nature. During my lifetime, I feel I have a kinship toward nature. In fact, you will see my name on the sign above the land in Myakka Park, because I wanted

Empty Nest

to be a part of Meg Loman's adventure in putting canopies all over the world.

It's important for people to appreciate the little things. It is noticing the little things and surrounding yourself with things that you're comfortable with. I have green in my house, because when I look out my window 17 stories high, and I see this beautiful green world, the palm trees, the live oaks. I just sit there and say, "We are so blessed."

I'm still an empty nester, but in the last two weeks, I've had my whole family with me twice. I went to see them on Mother's Day. We went up there because one of my granddaughters-in-law is expecting a baby any minute, and they couldn't get away from Tampa. Passover and Mother's Day and this week I was honored by Urban Meyer and Ohio State University with a big award from Alumni Association of Sarasota, which is the largest alumni group in the United States. I was with all my children three times in the last month. Thank God, and I could have been with them four times, because they went to California for Raymond's 70th. However, I couldn't go, because I have to be able to walk every hour for ten to twelve minutes and I can't do that on the plane.

When I'm with my four children, I'm cognizant of how special it is. We laugh a lot. Oh my God, I'm ready to burst.

This recent honor was for both me and Alex. Alex was honored posthumously and I felt like my husband was looking down on us smiling. Beautiful. The Urban Meyer event was a big-time honor.

I became active in the Women Builders of Charleston and with the Symphony Women. I was on the board and, of course, the board makes lots of decisions in terms of the master plans of the community.

They are all important. All these organizations that I got involved with are worldwide organizations and I love what they do for other people.

I also became active in the National Council of Jewish Women, which took Head Start from Israel and brought it to the United States. But the program falls short and it ends up not getting children ready for kindergarten. They're falling back. That's being changed, because I'm changing it. The federal government gave over 17 million dollars to improve HEAD START and they're doing it at Early Child Research School of Education at Ohio State. I gave one quarter of the money and the university gave three quarters and they named it after me.

I got involved in national and international organizations. I was very active in the Organization of Rehabilitation Training (ORT), which was established in 1880. The source of ORT was that Russia wanted Jews out of their country. So they would conscript for service boys of 14 years and older. A lot of Jewish people were trying to get out of the country, because they didn't want their 14-year-olds to serve and be used for cannon fodder. They weren't trained and they sent them in with guns as troops. There was a large migration to the United States. The Russians started trade schools for all their people, but the Jews were not allowed to go to those schools. Our ORT trade schools allow everyone to attend these schools. They became so respected that even until this day when people are looking for applicants for jobs, the job description often states, "ORT trained candidates preferred."

I actually got involved with ORT later in life. The Ethiopian Jews had a problem. They lived about 1200 feet above sea level and were farmers. They didn't own their own farms, but just leased them from the landholders. You paid them by farming the land and they gave half their crop to the land owners—the last half you were allowed to keep. You paid the landholder one quarter for the land and the other quarter you sold to live on yourself. They were able to farm, because they were up high and there were roots, dense woods, and plenty of rain up there. When the rains stopped in Africa, and there was a lull for years, they couldn't farm anymore, so they were literally starving. The land was barren—not productive. So those people were desperate to go somewhere. They lived in mud huts and had no sanitation.

They were given an education where they were taught to read and write for a year. They lived in homes that had no pencils, no paper, and no books. That was their education, which they never used. They climbed trees. When they climbed the steps of the airplane that took them to Israel, they had never been up a stair step in their life. They didn't know what a doorknob was. They took their wood on the plane to make their meals because they didn't how they would eat on an airplane. They were absolutely from another era.

My involvement with that group is as follows: I built a campus and I took and renovated their school, which was built in 1946. Everything was so decrepit in that school that they couldn't get a decent education. Nothing was in good working order. I completely redid the school and recently it was named by the Minister of Education as the best high school in the state of Israel today. The matriculation rate was 41 percent and 40 percent of those students were Russian and Ethiopian children and none of their parents had an education.

Emily and Betty have a conversation about her childhood days:

Betty: Emily, tell them good things. Don't tell them how I parked you at people's houses.

Emily: She left me out in the backyard to raise myself.

Betty: Don't tell them about the time I spanked you for dashing across the parking lot and almost getting killed. Don't tell them that.

Emily: Mother made dinner every night. We kind of had a revolving menu, like baked chicken with fresh green beans and sliced tomatoes. Good stuff. Meat sauce and spaghetti, chop suey from scratch, and then we would have an Israeli dish, or deviled eggs, and artichoke dips for parties.

When I would come home, Mom would be busy with her Mahjong group.

Betty: That's right—Betty Barrick, Sylvia Bedwinick, Ida Neurman, and me. It used to always be the same rules, but now the rules change every four years. I had played Maj down here, but it's been about 15 years. It's boring to me now.

Emily: I would get paid off in candy. I associate Mahjong with happy memories.

Betty: Tell them about your childhood and how I tried to make you a dancer and show you how to play the piano.

Emily: She tried to control me. I was an only child with siblings. I was young and have little memory.

Betty: What she's trying to say is that she didn't have too much communication with her brothers during that time.

Emil: We went to Virginia Beach and Hilton Head and I was the little play toy. And my cousins would bury me in the sand. I was like a prop.

Betty: They all paid attention to her, but she was too young to have any interaction.

Emily: You asked about some of the memories I had of growing up? There was juxtaposition between growing up the way we did and living around poverty. Many of my friends were very poor. It was in your face. People who didn't give back, didn't live there.

Mom even taught people how to give back. For Dad, it was competitive for him to do this. He would say, "Look what I've done" and "You mean you can't step up." For him, it wasn't so much a heart to heart thing, but more of a competitive thing.

Betty: I let your daddy give the money because he made it.

The Joy of Giving is the Joy of Living

Emily: But he made other people give by being competitive with them. He told them to put your name on it. Mom's approach was different and she would connect with your heart.

Betty: Your daddy was great at raising money.

Emily: When I see and feel my folks' philanthropy, it's nice. Each person who received a scholarship yesterday had their own stories of how Mom helped them specifically with what they needed. There was a woman who was going to school in her 50s. She talks about giving while you are living.

Betty: We gave ten scholarships away yesterday.

Emily: Well, there is a separation from the money. You know, that's what money does. We're not really proud of our money. It's just that it's a tool. Money is a tool. I don't think a lot of people grew up like we did. My dad was one of the few Jews, in Petersburg, Virginia, and they were beat up, as Jews, and that's what made them tough and good athletes.

Emily: What sports did Uncle Leon play?

Betty: He made the basketball and football teams and was the best athlete. Howard played baseball at Annapolis.

Emily: What about his brother, Raymond?

Betty: Raymond was a great sportsman, but he did all these things because he wanted to influence his brothers to get into sports. He died a hero in the war.

Emily: Uncle Raymond died in World War II? I didn't know that.

Betty: Alex and Raymond were 14 months apart. Raymond fought in Germany at the Battle of the Bulge. When Raymond passed away, a little part of your daddy died. Yes, sir, it affected him very much. It never left him. Alex felt that he had so much in life, a wife and children, and his brother Raymond had none of it. It affected his life. He asked himself, "Why should I have all this, when my brother didn't have any of it? There by the grace of God ... ."

Emily: What do I think that my folks' legacy is? It's not just writing checks. I know Mom's heart, because I have seen it. The same thread comes through whenever she talks—it's her heart. The Hug. All these things that shape her attitude. It's just a mother's way. It's not her words—it's just that people are drawn to her. I don't know why and she can't explain it. Phil King said this, "No matter how many times she speaks and stands there at the podium, it happens every time she speaks. Total silence. All eyes are on her. She draws attention." You better say something when you are up there.

(Emily and Betty laugh)

Betty: When I join an organization, I just don't write the check, I follow through and I get on their board and become involved. I want to be active and ensure that everything's going right with the organization.

Emily: There are things I don't know about Daddy, that were a mystery. When I was up in West Virginia, a guy who was about 40 years old came up to me at our bowling alley and said, "You're Alex's daughter. I probably wouldn't be here if it weren't for him. My mom was a single mom with three children at home. She was a Shoney's waitress and having a hard time getting us to school and getting herself to work on time. She told your dad her trials about how the bus was late and she was worried about getting fired. He told her, 'Where do you need to be and when, and I'll get you there.' So he would apparently drive her to work. He was a busy man running a large company, traveling a lot, but he helped in time of need."

The impact of touching people's lives is far greater than serving on a board. You see a need and you try to do what you can. He had a lot of skills. Some say I have a gene from both of them, but I don't have any of their skills.

I don't like to serve on boards. But I live in this world. I don't live in a bubble, because of where I grew up and because I've had the parents I've had. You can't separate that out, just because we had money. Maybe I wouldn't have gone to school if we didn't have money. We went to Europe, we traveled. I was exposed to a lot of intelligent people from different cultures. While I relate to a lot of what Mom and Dad have done, I have different interests. I have a Master's in Education.

Betty: Emily champions many causes—the environment, Planned Parenthood, hungry people, Thanksgiving dinner for the homeless.

Emily: People come to you and say, "The JCC has this Thanksgiving Day dinner every year, and this year they don't have a sponsor." If they don't cook that food and have the money to cook it, all these homeless people wouldn't get Thanksgiving dinner. You sit there and say, "Would I rather have the money in my bank account?"

The greatest thing about my parents is …

Betty whispers to Emily, "Say something nice."

Emily: I can't lump them together. But it's that she loves me. Unequivocally. He loved me, too. He was a quiet man. A very quiet man. Very succinct with his words. More a man of action than words.

Betty: He was tough.

Emily: Tough act to follow. Nobody's even tried it in this family. We all know that we can't do it. They're both a tough act to follow.

Betty: Remember, Emily, I didn't start till I was 79, so their time hasn't arrived yet.

Emily: You were doing stuff before you were 79.

Betty: Oh sure I was.

Emily: You ran for Homecoming Queen at Ohio State. You put yourself out there.

Betty: But I was Jewish and they'd never had a Jewish homecoming Queen. They asked me to do it.

Emily: It's a fascinating story, because her campaign manager became Ambassador to India. And it was her only failure.

Betty: I lost because there were only three Jewish fraternities that voted for me. Now the Gentiles didn't vote for me, so I had to ask the Jews. And we could only date those three Jewish fraternities from our sororities and they said they were the only good ones on campus. It was terrible then. Dirty, dirty, dirty. I dated a boy from another fraternity and they were going to blackball me, if I didn't stop going with him. (Laughs) I knew I wasn't going to win. The Gentile people weren't going to vote for me and I didn't care, because I knew I would not get elected. I was on the court. Anybody who ran was on the court.

Emily: What was your homecoming Queen slogan?

Betty: Betty Frank will make a better Queen than Wally Simpson.

We made light that Wally Simpson was like Wallis Simpson—a commoner in line to be the Duchess of Windsor, when King Edward abdicated the British Crown and chose marriage instead of being King.

Betty and Emily laugh.

Empty Nest

Betty: Emily was my last child, and when she left home, my nest was empty. But one thing about Emily—when I need her help, she always comes back to the nest.

Chapter 18

Losing Her All-American

"Loss doesn't feel redeemable. But for me one consoling aspect is the recognition that, in this at least, none of us is different from anyone else: We all lose loved ones; we all face our own death."

— Meghan O'Rourke

Alex passed away on December 6, 1996.

He was terribly ill, but he didn't tell anybody. He never complained. My husband never complained when he was sick. He was in denial all the time. He had diabetes and when he drank a little too much scotch, he would just take more insulin in the morning. He denied it all and never tested his sugar. If he felt a little bad he would just take a little more insulin.

He didn't watch his diet like I did and he loved ice cream. Coffee was his favorite flavor. He didn't have a lingering illness where he was bed-ridden and was active right up to the time he passed. He was honored on a Saturday night.

And he was in the hospital with oxygen because of his breathing.

I knew Alex for 61 years of my life.

I met Alex when I was 17, a week from 18 and I was 79 when he passed away. I knew him 61 years and yes, I did know him better than anyone. Better even than his own mother and father, because they didn't want to see some of the things that Alex was.

He had the kind of father who when Alex wanted to go in the restaurant business said, "What the hell do you know about the restaurant business? Why would you go into that? You're going to lose a lot of money. Go into something you know about."

My husband would make his case, "Pop, give them good high quality food, a pleasant environment, and good service and you can sell food. It's promotion that's important. And you know I'm good at promotion." Alex was great at promotion.

I encouraged him because I could see his potential. His father was always afraid that Alex would embarrass him and he didn't want him to be a failure. So then when my husband would get involved with something, his father would say, "I bet you can't do it." In other words, he wanted to challenge him, because he didn't want him to become a failure. So my husband would always go into something saying, "My daddy says I can't do it."

Well, he never mentioned this to me, but I knew—I could tell. And I would say finally, "Alex, don't go into things to satisfy your father, but you do it to satisfy yourself. Don't do things if your father challenges you to do something and don't do it because he wants you to succeed so he can proud. That isn't what a father should do. He should encourage you, to do whatever you want to do and say to you, 'Son, try it. If you don't make it, you will have learned a lesson.' And that's the best way to get successful. To learn your lessons and don't do it again."

One of the sweet memories, I think one of the things that I really enjoyed about my husband, was that he was a giver. He gave not only of his financial help, but also his time to help raise money. He was the head of many campaigns, where he raised a lot of money. As I mentioned, he raised 31 million dollars for the Salvation Army to give them a pension plan, because they had little money for the retirement of their employees. He saw that they had a problem and did something about it. They came to him and told him they had problems and he told them that he would raise that money in five years with only one professional helper that would handle all the money. He didn't want to have anything to do with the money. He was so honest that he didn't want anybody thinking that he was keeping some of the money. They sent him a professional who handled the money and Alex had to see every check that was sent to the bank. My husband had a lot of integrity and honor. His handshake and his word. That was another generation. At that time, a handshake would be your word. We didn't have all these lawyers. (Laughs)

The thing I miss most about him is getting into bed at night and having his arm around me while I'm sleeping. He always put his arm around my waist and we'd cuddle. (Smiles)

We cuddled. And cuddling was what it's all about.

The love that we had for each other was wonderful.

The business was everything to him. No, really. The business was everything first. I mean, once he started the business, I already had two children. He knew that I was busy taking care of the kids, so all his attention went toward the business.

Whenever I wanted to give some money away, my husband never objected. But after he passed away, I was empowered with all this money that he had been giving away for years. I had to learn a lot. I learned about the stock market and so much about business that I never knew before, because my husband never believed that women should be in the business world. He was born in Richmond, Virginia, where southern women like "his mother" didn't work.

I've had wonderful children. They all have big hearts, because their daddy was a giver and so was I. That's what they learned growing up—giving. And they give.

My biggest challenge was that my husband came from a family of four boys. He thought that women could not be business people. He did not share with me the intricacies of the business. Now, I'm not stupid, so I could see the business growing and growing and growing. I could see and read our statements every year. I knew what was happening. But I knew nothing about business, because he didn't let me in on anything. In fact, after he passed away, I was on the Foundation Board at Ohio State University and one day I got up in front of the whole board and told them that,

"Men are too macho. They think that women should stay home and take care of the children, cook, and take care of the home."

I did everything—I took care of all the checks for the house and the utilities. I knew that part, the business part of running a home. But I didn't know the business part of running a business. At 79, I received the estate. I didn't know much about the stock market. Women back then didn't learn, like the women nowadays who attend stockbroker meetings.

The lesson is: "Let your wife know what is happening in your life, so that when you pass away, they are not lost."

I now go into nursing homes and adult living facilities and I ask some women for a contribution like the $5,000 I gave when my husband was alive. But she won't give the $5,000, because she says, "My husband died and I won't have enough money to live on." Some of these women are wealthier now than they were when their husbands were alive, but they don't understand. They're older and their minds are not as good so they just won't donate any money.

Still the hardest part was the loss of my husband—the vacancy. I mean going to bed at night by myself and not having to get up in the morning to feed my husband. I mean, you realize what a pleasure it was before and that you can't do it anymore.

I didn't have much mourning time. I didn't have much time to think about it, because I had to get in there and start working. I had to, because things were always pending that I had to do. It was a big adjustment. I had to learn especially when it comes to investments. If you have never invested, and I did, I was pretty smart, because I got some of the top stocks at that time and I've done very well with them. My husband had sold three companies to Marriot and they paid him in stock. And that was fabulous stock. I didn't get advice on all this. I just got it through my head, when I saw how well Marriot was doing. I just kept my Marriot stock.

Socially? My husband wasn't that social. He had his friends. We had couples that we knew. He loved sports and used to watch sports on television. His male friends would usually come to his office and talk to him. In fact, he loved that. When he became chairman of the board, which is not as important as running the business, he had time to sit and kibitz. In fact, he changed his office three times until he found a building where the people were friendly. In other words, in other buildings, people had to work. In his building were a bunch of men, who needed an office, where they would probably go to relax and sleep on the sofa. (Laughs) He went to work every day. The building he liked best is the building where the University Club was on Main Street. But they wanted him to wear a tie at lunch, so he stopped going.

He was not a bridge player. He was all business. We had a lot of parties, usually for an occasion like a birthday, anniversary, or something for the Temple or Synagogue. I gave a lot of parties. In fact, I bought this big place, because in the beginning, I gave so many parties, but not now. In fact, I ought to sell this place, because everybody wants to have a party up here. It's great house for a party.

Alex never lived here and he would not have lived here. He didn't like heights. Well, I didn't think I would like heights either, but when I came up and saw this view, it didn't bother me at all. The only thing that worries me is if there is a fire, I would have to go down 17 flights of stairs, because the elevator isn't used during a fire. I hope to God, I don't have to do that.

Alex and I used to play golf and Mahjong all the time, but when I had Emily, I wanted to be a good mom and as good a mother as I was to my other children, especially when Emily was an infant. So I gave up Mahjong and golf and I haven't played since then.

Alex wasn't a big talker. He was a thinker. It wasn't companionship—it is just that I loved him and that we were together.

We had a wonderful family and they gave me a lot of pleasure. They were active in sports, football, basketball, track, and rowing. I went to all the games and meets. We just had a wonderful family.

Alex was a perfectionist. I'm not a perfectionist. I'd like it to be perfect, but know that you can't make everything perfect. A good example of Alex being a perfectionist is when our waitresses would come in to work. The rule was no chewing gum.

I'm chewing gum right now, because I have no saliva and I couldn't talk to you without it. My mother told me nice girls don't chew gum. That's why when I put a piece of gum into my mouth, I feel guilty, because I have to chew.

Alex was tough with our sons. When they wanted to go into something, he would say, "I bet you can't do it." It was his way of motivating them. Same as his dad. My way of motivating them was to tell them they could achieve anything they wanted to, if they set their heart to it. Any mistake you make is a lesson and one that you won't do again. Each lesson you learn makes you smarter. If you have a detour, you get on the road again. Alex and I were Ying and Yang.

I'm not the same person at all that I was before Alex passed away. I didn't know that I had some of the qualities I had until he passed and I became my own person.

For example, I've had good luck influencing other people to give. Many people come up to me and say, "I went to an event where you spoke. I will never forget your words." They quote my words to me and say, "You have triggered my desire to give."

I am a different person and didn't know that I had this power in me to give a speech and influence people to give. People stop me on the street and tell me that because of me, they give.

When did I know I had that power? Well, it took me a while. I didn't know I had it, until they asked me to speak in Palm Beach to a group of women, most of whom were all worth ten million dollars or more. One of these groups spoke of how we pass our values on to the next generation. They asked me to come and speak, so I spoke. I could see that the people there were leaning over waiting for my next word. I couldn't believe it! I had these people spellbound. Jane Pauley spoke the night before and didn't get a standing ovation. That morning after I spoke, the first time that I ever did, I got a standing ovation when I was finished. Then after the Question and Answer period, I got another standing ovation. By that time, I had to go to the bathroom. It was in the morning and I had been talking all morning, so I dashed off the stage to the bathroom and nobody was in there. Two minutes later, they closed the meeting and everybody was in there. I was in one of those stalls, and I was so embarrassed, because they were talking about how marvelous and wonderful I was and here I was—in the bathroom stall. I just stayed in that bathroom until everybody left!

That was a Eureka moment.

Another time shortly after that I went up to Charleston, West Virginia, where they were raising money for United Way and they made me a mister—like Mr. Rogers. They gave me a rocking chair and put a quilt on it, and something to place my hat on and a place to take my shoes off. I was sitting up on stage and people were coming up and talking to me. I influenced those people. At the end of the talk, I did a terrific thing. I made everybody hug each other. After that I told everybody to put their arms in the air and reach up, as high as they can and just stay there for five seconds and, please, everyone be quiet. Then I said reach for heaven and feel the power there is in this room to change the world. Oh my God, the applause I got after that. It was amazing how you can move people and that I had this power.

It comes from a real place. Like my secretary Ray says, "Mrs. Schoenbaum doesn't make a speech—she just stands up there and speaks from her heart." That's the most effective thing in the world. You don't look down at a speech. You don't hesitate. Your English might not be as good as you would put in a speech, but you get the message across. People stop me on the street and tell me that I changed their life. The other day at the Asolo Theatre, a woman came over to me and said, "Are you Betty Schoenbaum?" She had attended something at the Van Wezel, heard me speak, and said that I had changed her life and that her life has become so much richer and wonderful.

I still like giving speeches. I love the opportunity, because I know I can help charities and I still feel I can do this, because I've got all my marbles.

I was very heavy into non-profit women's organizations. When I was with my children, I was with Girl and Boy Scouts. PTAs. But I became more of a leader and voice after Alex passed.

Another thing that I have done since Alex died is give away a lot of money. Lots and lots of money. I have a foundation in Charleston, where all the money that I gave there has to go to the Kanawha Valley. I can't take that money and give it down here. Then I have money that I give to foundations. Locally, I have my own private foundation—the Schoenbaum Family Foundation. My husband used to give all the money from that foundation away all by himself. When he passed away, that money was handed over to me. What I've done is I want to teach my children how to give, so I asked them if I could have half of that money. It was mine, so I didn't have to ask them. I could have just done it, but I wanted to be fair so I told them. "I would like to take half the money and give it to the things that your daddy has been giving to, because he loves those causes, and I'd like to give the rest of it away to the causes that I believe in. The other half, I will give you each a quarter of it, and you will learn how to give. You will learn to look up a charity in Charity Navigator and find out which ones really spend the money on what they're supposed to and not on high salaries, fancy offices and expensive advertising.

Here is my advice with money and giving.

After you take care of your own needs, there are so many causes that you could give to that are run beautifully and have an impact on people's lives. That's what you should do with your money.

My big thing is education. Other causes that I like to give to are helping the homeless, but they've been wrangling over homelessness for two years in Sarasota and they haven't done enough.

I have so many big projects all over the world. I started a project in Israel and I gave them five million dollars for a school, a soccer field, and a running track like the Olympic track.

The biggest change when Alex was not with me was learning the business world. Settling the estate was a big job. Most of the money was passed down to me. I gave my children enough money to build the house of their dreams. I thought, "Why should I give them money when I die, because I'll never see those houses. And when I die, they may not need the houses. Now they really need the houses. They have young children and everything. Raymond was really the only one who built the house of his dreams, but I think maybe before I'm gone, I'll get to see the others live in the houses of their dreams—their dream houses. Because I feel you should give your money where you can see what good your money is doing. Don't give when you die, because you don't know where that money is going and if they use it for what you specified.

"There are no luggage racks on a hearse. You can't take it with you. You might as well give it right now to see where it's going. Have that joy in your life and that joy helps you live longer."

After Alex passed, a world that Alex didn't share with me opened up. I knew he did well. I knew how much he made, because I used to help sign the tax returns. But I don't think I was impressed with how well he did, especially because everything I needed I got. What's the difference of how much it is? We always had enough and always did what we wanted to do.

Did I have regrets in not knowing? Well, perhaps now that I know that I was capable of being more of a help to my husband, if he would have taken it.

Accumulating wealth allows you to help the family and to be able to help so many. Fortunately, my family really didn't need the money, except my youngest daughter. I was concerned about Emily, because she wasn't married yet. I thought that God forbid, she should have some sickness where she needs help all the time when she is older. So in my will, I gave my youngest daughter more money than the others. My two sons have made their money themselves without their daddy's help and my daughter, Joann, is married to a very successful dermatologist. They have plenty to leave to their children. I was in a different position. My children are going to get some of my money when I pass away.

I felt like I had enough to share with the rest of the world, so that I could change it, if I would plan careful projects and contribute to them.

I picked up the philanthropy torch after my husband's passing. He was a big philanthropist. I recovered pretty well during that time when I lost him, because I was so busy that I didn't suffer like some women have.

It wasn't a mourning period. But you do miss the little things.

Today I see Alex as a man who cared tremendously about others. He was really wrapped up in his business, because he thought nobody could run it as well he did.

In 1996, I started getting involved with the nonprofits mostly for women and education. I'm doing it, because I wanted to carry the torch that my husband carried. To this day, I'm partial to things he gave to, like the Boys Club, the Salvation Army, Ohio State University, the Jewish Family, Children's Service, and several more. I'm still partial to those causes, because I knew that if Alex were here, he would be giving to them.

I was so busy I didn't even know what I was doing. I met with lawyers, estate planners, trying to learn everything.

I was always confident in myself, having been a performer and getting up in front of people and speaking. I grew so much during that period. With all the planning I did back then, I realized maybe I would have been a good business woman. But I'm glad I didn't do that, because I wouldn't have had times to help all these women's organizations and raise a family.

I think I was a very good mother. That's very important. My children know that I love them. I just read something this morning that stated, "What's lacking in education is the parent's love of their children. They don't have the basics." That's why you should hug your children. Hug your children to let them know that you love them.

I really took care of mine. I never had a cook ever, although I had one girl who made wonderful fried chicken. I cooked all the meals myself. I never had anybody pick my children up for me. I didn't have extra help, because I enjoyed doing it for my children.

I had cooked from the time I was 22 until I was 79. Alex was content and easy to suit. If you had a bowl of soup and some good bread, he'd rather stay in and eat that, than go out and have a big dinner at Euphemia Haye, which was right across the street. He preferred to stay home. In fact, there was a little shack on Bradenton Beach with the best apple walnut pie in the world. He would prefer going there than any fancy restaurant.

With his loss, I didn't get lonely, because I had a lot of friends from West Virginia down here that lived on Longboat. They were wonderful at keeping me busy. When you have someone whom you have known for 50 years and they reach out, it's a wonderful feeling that you have this wonderful anchor.

I wasn't the same person I was when I met Alex and when he passed away. My God, I'm another person entirely. I grew so much. I guess I was sheltered before having two of the most wonderful parents in the world. They let you do what you thought was right for you, and they cared about you tremendously. I'll tell you, I look back on my life and I think that I have been so blessed with family, the greatest parents, a husband who knew where he was going and he got there, and it seems that my life has always been up, up, and up.

I was seldom depressed—not even after losing Alex. I didn't have time to be depressed. I was learning too much and it was just overwhelming. I didn't have time to pity myself. I was always too busy.

I have said, "Don't sit down, because you might not get back up." It's all about getting involved in life.

What I like to do is take a person and give them a scholarship and see how they turn out. It's such a wonderful feeling. If they get any awards, you feel like if I didn't help them with their education, they may not have gotten that award. You feel so good about what you do, when you help other people.

It excites me. Oh my gosh!

Many times, someone comes up to me and says, "Are you Betty Schoenbaum?" When I say, "Yes," they continue, "You gave me a chance and now I'm head of forensics at the county jail."

Imagine a woman coming up to you and saying that she wouldn't be where she was today, if you didn't give her that money for four years of college. It was nothing really. Not a lot of money—$1000 a year for a scholarships at Manatee Community College.

It's an obligation. To ensure you have enough for yourself, figure the two percent cost of living increase for as many years as you think you might live. I figured up to 100 years of age. I had a nice amount of money put away and now I'm getting to close to being 100.

Over the last decade it's been a little bit more of a challenge, because of my health. Only the last couple of years I've been a little depressed about my condition, but not badly depressed, maybe for five minutes. It's not a long depression, because I keep myself busy.

I am so overbooked. That's why I look forward to those gems of free time. There aren't very many. I'm always hurrying. The phone rings. My life is busy.

It's something that I say I would like to change about myself, but when I do have an empty day, I feel like my life is empty. So there you are. That's the honest truth.

When Alex passed away, naturally the hardest part was missing him, because we had been married 56 years and I had gone with him for 5 years before I married him. I knew him for 61 years of my 79.

If you keep busy, it's not as bad, as if you stay home and feel sorry for yourself. I'm one of these people who like to be with others, so I don't think it was that difficult for me.

Betty's father as child

*Betty's mother and daddy courting
Dayton, Ohio*

*Two sisters -
Betty Schoenbaum age one with sister Gerri*

Dancing School /Dayton, Ohio

Betty the Bathing Beauty Crystal Lake, Ohio 1945

*The Summer Cottage Crystal Lake, Ohio, 1938
Betty, Mother and Alex*

*Betty & Alex Schoenbaum
Graduation day from The Ohio State University*

Betty Schoenbaum with Alex Schoenbaum & his mom, dad and brothers during World War II.

Grandma Fannie Goldman with Betty & siblings WWII

The Frank's Family Home - Dayton, Ohio

Betty and Alex Schoenbaum, California. 1957

Alex and Betty Schoenbaum

The Alex Schoenbaum Family
Alex, Betty, Raymond, Jeffry & Joann 1962

*Betty's 85th Birthday with her Four Children
Kanawha River, Charleston, West Virginia*

Betty Schoenbaum still in fashion showing off legs at 89 years of age

Betty Schoenbaum & Kay Glasser Human Service Center, 1998

*Betty & Alex Schoenbaum with
West Virginia Senator Jay Rockefeller.*

*Schoenbaum Hall–Undergraduate School of Business
The Ohio State University Campus Columbus, Ohio*

Adam Schoenbaum Family Wedding
"The Family" that Alex and Betty Started
Ritz Carlton Lodge, Georgia 2014

Betty and her love of hats

Betty Schoenbaum Charleston, West Virginia, 2004

The Schoenbaum Family Thanksgiving Day, 1995 Longboat Key, Florida

Betty and Big Boy

Betty with daughter Emily

The Grand Lady – Betty Schoenbaum
Sarasota, Florida 2017

Betty Schoenbaum's descendents

100th Birthday –Sarasota, Florida

Part Four

Betty's New Life Without Her Big Boy

Chapter 19

Philanthropy Takes Center Stage

"Charity is just writing checks and not being engaged. Philanthropy, to me, is being engaged, not only with your resources but getting people and yourself really involved and doing things that haven't been done before."

— Eli Broad

"He who opens a school door, closes a prison."

—Victor Hugo

With the loss of her soulmate, sure, Betty felt sad and alone at times. And sometimes her friend, the piano, kept her balanced. But the greater goal, the greater purpose, seldom allowed this woman named Betty Schoenbaum to feel sorry for herself. There was too much to do and too many people to help. The letter B in her first name could have easily stood for busy, because this great lady, now approaching 80, was busier than ever. She had to be. There were worthy causes to help lend her name and dollars to and, of course, there were people to help.

With this great lady from Dayton, it was always about helping people, starting first with her family, then with the family of mankind. And one other thing that Betty had always been cognizant of was just how important it was to give of yourself to others, in any way you can give. And, of course, there are hugs to give and the art of hugging is a lesson she gladly gives one-on-one to anyone blessed to be within hugging distance.

In learning this lesson of giving, Betty was tutored by two of the best mentors and teachers. First lessons on giving were taught to her as a child by her granny, Fanny Goldman. Then later, by a boy she met on the first day of school, and with whom she spent a good part of her life, her soulmate Alex from Virginia with the big heart, she lived the giving lessons. When Alex passed away, he passed the torch of giving to her. This is something she holds on to with great pride and responsibility, knowing that Alex's spirit is still guiding her giving ways from the other side. This is a secret that Betty knows all too well, as she fills her appointment book with people and organizations to help. She knows that she is not alone in her giving. Betty knows that both Granny Goldman and Alex are still looking down to see all the good that she can do with each and every day that she is blessed to be given by the Creator—the greatest teacher of them all.

Education is the most important thing in this country, especially now. It costs a lot of money to send our children to school—even to our public schools. When you think of it, if you don't give a child a good education, and they can't read well by the third grade, they're never going to able to read well and get through school. To keep a felon in a penitentiary, it costs $52,000 a year. Do you want to spend $9,200 for a good education or do you want to pay $52,000 a year to keep them in the penitentiary for the rest of their lives?

Something I'm so excited about, education-wise, is helping childhood education, starting at zero. You can teach in the womb. I have a research school at Ohio State University.

I started this around ten years ago in the latter part of my life. Three blocks from the gates of Ohio State University, there was a neighborhood called Weinland Park. The population was made up of 75% prostitutes and 25% drug and alcohol addicts. They were noted for murders on Friday and Saturday nights. It was called Tent City, because the housing was horrible. Well, urban development went down there and improved it, put a cap on the rent, and told people they can't tear it down and build something new. I put a 40,000 square foot school in there that eventually cost $10 million dollars that is big for Urban Childhood Education from ages zero to five years.

This was a terrible and horrible area. The federal government gave the program that we started at Ohio State $13,350,000 for the next five years to improve Head Start, which was not preparing children for kindergarten. These children fell behind in kindergarten, because the other children that they mixed with had better preparation for kindergarten. Head Start is not working. And *our* program is helping 4,200 families in the central part of Ohio by giving them better programming.

I'm bursting with pride and joy, because we're doing something about keeping children in school. In this program, they took women who were pregnant in this terrible neighborhood and asked them not to play their rap music, but to play Mozart's lullabies every night instead. They were told to keep the music soft, like background music, but not harsh like rap music. They did that for six months and then, they took the music away from them and they weren't exposed to it until they were born. Then they brought their babies into the lab, placed them into real baby beds and put a monitor on each baby's heart. Next, they turned the classical music on and the children's eyes lit up like stars. Their feet kicked, their hands clapped, and their hearts pounded, because they were hearing their music again. You learn in the womb.

I'm still learning today. I get inspired by speakers. When I think about education, I think about children. My program teaches Respect, Reliance, and Responsibility, knowing how to keep their mouths shut in school, being respectful to other children in school, and not bullying. It teaches all that. When a child gets all that, they build self-esteem. When they have self-esteem, they won't do wrong things, because they like themselves.

Those three R's are more important than the traditional 3 R's taught in school. What's the sense of teaching them Reading, Writing, and Arithmetic, if they're going to be rude children?

In terms of my own grandchildren, I do see them often. They're all grown up with my great-grandchildren. I see them all. I even have one great-grandchild in the womb right now. He's coming out in June. (Smiles) Just having another baby. We just had another one, Nate. He's my oldest son's grandson.

And my oldest son, Raymond, will be 70 in April. God has blessed me with ineffable joy.

What would I like to leave the new baby? This book I'm writing to teach my children the kind of life you can live if you give.

The joy of giving is the joy of living.

I don't tell them anything. They've learned already. If they don't learn it at home, they don't learn it. What I want to tell them is to be good citizens. To share. To be faithful.

It's good to be curious about things I'm curious about. Some things I couldn't give a darn for. I'm especially involved in people and how people get out of situations they're in when they are underprivileged.

A light has to go off in me. There are so many groups in need. I give to the arts very generously usually through my endowments. Sometimes I will give by attending their parties.

The key is I give to organizations or causes I'm passionate about. I am passionate about the arts. I studied ballet for 15 years. So naturally I give to that wonderful institution, the Ballet and Florida Studio Theatre. I want it to stay there, so I give to them. I think our orchestra is absolutely fabulous, so I've endowed them. I have scholarships at Ringling College of Art, because I think it's one of the greatest in the country. The arts are important to me, because I love them. I love to go to concerts, ballets, and plays, so I support them, so that they will continue to be here. I think the arts are about history. They play music like that of Tchaikovsky or Mozart. We must continue to support them, because it's a culture that we don't want to lose.

In terms of major giving, I didn't really get involved until Alex passed away and I came into the funds that he had been giving away. I was giving major contributions in my categories for what women were giving, but nothing like what Alex gave. He would give a million dollars away and I have given away a million dollars myself now. Back then the house came first. The home. I did not miss a thing, because I was happy doing what I was doing.

I was a mother first. Housewife second. And I was proud of that. I had wonderful kids. If you want a good family, you have to work at it. It just doesn't happen. You're home for your children when you have to be home. I know a lot of women have to work now, because the salaries are not what they used to be. It takes two to run a household. Until they raise the minimum wage, we're going to have no middle class people anymore. It will be the very rich and the very poor.

In our household, we never discussed charities. Alex never asked me. We never had an argument over what he was going to give, because I loved everything he gave to. Alex was a marvelous giver—a wonderful role model in terms of giving and philanthropy.

He didn't care what I thought, yet his thoughts were the same as mine. I do believe there are two types of people in the world—givers and takers. Definitely, I'm a giver. But I'm also a taker, because of the joy I get from giving—I'm a taker of the joy.

I do believe that you get more from giving. Oh my God. It's unbelievable. Unbelievable. It's ineffable joy. Joy beyond description.

I grew into this role after motherhood when all the carpooling was over. When your children go to Hebrew School, you pick up three or four children and we took turns during the week. One picks them up one week, another picks them up another week. Carpool.

Back in the day, when I was a mom, I was quite busy carting children everywhere, as some moms are doing today. Others are not doing it, because they're working. I was taking my boys to football practice and I had a job doing it. By the time I had Emily, the boys were in college, but when I had Joann, she was ten years younger. I had to get her up from her naps and schlep here and there. Then I had to get the boys to football practice and dentist appointments, braces for their teeth, and everything.

I didn't worry about energy. I was young. I had energy. I wish I had it now. The carpooling wasn't finished until I was 67! When I was 64, my daughter Emily got her driver's license I didn't have to car pool anymore. I started carpooling at 28 and I'd take them everywhere. By 64, I was DONE. Most women are finished by 45 or 50. So I wasn't as busy driving, but you're a mother all your life.

Finally, I had some time. Freedom! Freedom! (Laughs) I don't have to be anyplace at a certain time. I became involved with organizations. Even recently I just joined more organizations.

One of the great organizations that we got involved with

was the Salvation Army. When my brother-in-law who was killed in the Battle of the Bulge came off the battlefield and got to the Salvation Army, he was served hot soup and sandwiches. Alex's brother, Raymond, was killed in that battle by American fire. They were fighting head to head when they were bombed from the air. They couldn't tell who was an American and who was a German, so tragically Alex's brother was killed.

Because of that letter from my brother-in-law at the front, I never gave a cent to another organization, which I won't mention by name, but who didn't treat my brother-in-law and the men fighting with what I felt was the proper dignity. The Salvation Army treated him with dignity and I never forgot that and neither did Alex.

All my life I've weighed every place where I gave money and watched how they allocated their dollars. I got involved and became very active. My philosophy is simple. "If I'm going to give money to them, I want to know all about them. I want to know who the head of the organization is. I want to know where the money is going. I want to know what they're accomplishing. I won't give money until I know that."

I gave a scholarship this week to The National Council of Jewish Women, so they would have a few scholarships to give. A woman there who got a scholarship stood up and started talking and mentioned my name, Betty Schoenbaum. She said, "Betty Schoenbaum helped me get my first scholarship at the Women's Resource Center. From that, I became a certified nurse's assistant. Then I made enough money to go at night and become a registered nurse. Now I'm working on my master's degree in nursing. Hopefully after that, I will become a PhD and I will be able to teach other people nursing."

If I hadn't given a girl that first $1000 dollars for school to get her CNA, she may never have gotten to where she did. She was a beautiful black woman with poise who had everything.

Sometimes I am surprised at these events, because I didn't know what happened to her after I gave her the money. The feeling in my heart? You just feel so blessed that you were able to do it. I was dancing on clouds. I was, honest to God. Even when I tell it to you, you can see my feeling. Joy.

It's like when you throw a stone in a pond and you see it ripple, but you don't know how far the impact will be. That's right. That's why this year I am giving out ten, one thousand-dollar scholarships at the Women's Resource Center.

Am I blessed? I care. That's why I do it. I invest in people. In caring. I really care about these folks very much. A lot of these women I give scholarships to don't have a spouse, but they have children. They work. They go to school. They raise their children.

Is it tougher today for a woman? Oh, my God, yes. The woman that I gave it to today has four children, 14, 10, 8, and 16 months. She is going to school and maintaining her home. I didn't hear about a husband. We didn't talk about a husband. This woman is Angela Koblan, the 2016 recipient. We make the check out to the school that they are attending. We don't give them the money to spend on themselves. It goes right toward the tuition.

It's very important and is the responsibility of the giver to know where they are giving. You need to know what the receiving organization is going to do with your money. There is a book out there called *Charity Navigator*. If you have a non-profit, you must send all your information in to the IRS. How much does the organization take in and how much do they spend. Unfortunately, some of these organizations that we think sound so wonderful if you look them up in the Charity Navigator you find that most of them are Four F. That's the lowest rating you can get.

In some cases contributions pay for fancy offices and they give themselves big salaries. Some use expensive advertisements to get the money and much of the funds go for that, while only maybe 10 or 20 percent goes for the organization's mission.

That's why you must check them out. I'm really proud of projects like Glasser-Schoenbaum. That organization is close to my heart. That's a big one. It is a non-profit, with currently 19 non-profits under one big roof with many different buildings encompassing 60,000 square feet. We do not make a cent on the rent. The Salvation Army is there and we have a big clinic for the Health Department, a children's clinic that covers children from zero to 18 who do not have health insurance or cash. It is a place where parents or caretakers can bring their children to get healthcare.

It was set up by Dr. Kay Glasser. All we did was give them a half a million dollars to start the project and they got a consortium of banks to give them money. They gave it to them at 2% interest and we got the land for $1 for five and half acres for 99 years. The land was contaminated, so we had to clean that up. We have 12,500 visits a month from people coming through there. Sometimes the same people come three or four times a week. In the course of a year, we have over a million people coming through there. Still many people don't know about it.

My husband thought it was a good idea to have all these various agencies under one roof. They could go from housing to health to services that help those who are blind or perhaps homeless. Many things are taken care of there. Legal services are offered for free or little money. Glasser Schoenbaum makes me feel proud. It's a mall of human services.

Another organization I'm extremely proud of is the JFCS. With the JFCS, 80 percent of their clients are nondenominational and are not Jewish. That's the slogan of Judaism—"To Heal the World." The world is made up of many more Christians and other religions. It's up to us to heal the world—and we do! We take care of veterans, the homeless and those who are hungry. We help with their rent. We do so much for them. We help them find jobs. We have a couple of hundred volunteers, most of whom have excellent educations. They are retired, so they come to our organization to help.

I still feel Alex's presence, even today. Whenever I give a big gift to anything, I say to him, "I think you'll like that Alex," because he gave to everything.

The Salvation Army is a big one for me, because that was a big one for Alex. In five years, he raised 31.5 million dollars by having people come to Shoney's for free breakfast at 7:30 in the morning. He went to all the Shoney's all over the southeast and invited the wealthiest people in town to that breakfast. At first not many came, but five years later there wasn't enough room in the restaurant to put the people, because they all wanted to help.

When I think of that story I look up to the heavens and I can see him winking down at me, "I did good Alex." I'm very proud of the Salvation Army—I'm on the board and every year, I give an award in his name.

Chapter 20

Hugs

"There's a long life ahead of you and it's going to be beautiful, as long as you keep loving and hugging each other."

— Yoko Ono

Hugging—I started hugging heart-to-heart a couple years ago. It all started with the treatment of Israel and how they begged the world to join them and help them get rid of the terrorists. And nobody came to help. Nobody. Not a person in the world. When others are in trouble, we send a lot of help, but when Israel is in trouble, no one comes to help. We bought that land from the Palestinians. The Palestinians. Mohammad never came to Israel ever. Of course it was Palestine then, but he never came to Palestine. But Palestine belongs to them, because Mohammad said so? Do you really think Mohammad said that? He never went there, so how would he know what he's asking for? It's says in the Koran that he never went there.

So when Israel asked for help no one helped.

People don't love any more. People don't care anymore. I decided that a love hug is what the world needs, because you have to spread it around the world. When you hug a person heart-to-heart with a sincere hug, it's a heart hug, which is different than any other hug. It's sort of a love hug. Okay? I hug you. A hug raises your endorphins and helps your autoimmune system. It's a gift that you can give and you don't want to exchange it. Not only that, but you have it forever. I think it's a wonderful thing to spread around. You should hug your family. Hug your friends. Hug a stranger who is lonesome sometime. It will mean so much to them.

We have so much hate in the world, we have got to have some kind of love. Can it solve some things in the world? I think it makes you feel better. Anything that makes you feel better in these times that we're having in this world, well, it's a wonderful thing to hug heart-to-heart.

If I had someone from Islam, someone from the Jewish state, a Christian, and a Hindu at my table, I would hug every one of them. And I would have them hug each other. We all descended from Abraham, Isaac, and Jacob. We are brothers all over the world. When we go to war, we are killing our brothers, and when somebody cuts off somebody's head, it's their brother they are hurting.

I hug everybody. When I see a saleslady and see how harassed she may be, and I say, "Wait a minute, I'm going to give you a hug." And it calms people down.

Hugs are good. When I hug children, I just get down on their level and hug them. A love hug.

I'm going to give you a hug. Heart-to-heart. Keep your eyes closed. Lower your hands very slowly and drop your shoulders. And have your arms reach for the floor and your

Hugs

fingers will start tingling. This raises your endorphins and increases your autoimmune system.

When you are in stress and have no one to hug, hug yourself. When you give yourself a hug, it works just as good as when you get one from someone else.

Hugs help you have a beautiful day.

And every one of my days is beautiful.

I'm alive.

Chapter 21

My Piano/Art & Artifacts

"If music be the food of love, play on."

— William Shakespeare

The piano. It's my psychiatrist.

When I sit at the piano, I can forget about everything.

That someone is coming over to do an interview, or that I have to be someplace at twelve o'clock today and 4 pm later today, and 6:30 tonight. When I don't want to think about those things, I play the piano.

I started playing the piano when I was eight years old.

I did not have a natural talent for that instrument. My sister took violin and my mother thought I should take the piano, so we could play duos. That's why I took it up. My teacher was Miss Fredricks, who was a very strict. When I was 16 years old, she gave me Rimsky-Korsakov's, *The Bumble Bee,* to play as my recital piece.

She kept telling me that I was playing the wrong notes and I told her I can't help it. She told me that my fingernails are too long and that I had to cut them. I said, "I quit." So I quit playing at 16, because my fingernails had to be cut. I played it all the time throughout my life for the same reason I play it today. It's my psychiatrist. When I want to escape from anything I just sit down at that piano and play all my recital pieces like the *The Bumble Bee*, Beethoven's *Fur Elise* or *The Blue Danube* by Strauss, just to name a few.

I escape through playing music, but don't play often, because I just don't have the time. (Laughs)

I wasn't really encouraged by my parents to play, other than my mother wanting me to play, because my sister played violin. Since we were dancers who danced together, my mother thought that we could play the piano and violin in our act. Mother thought I should be the pianist. That's how I took up the piano. I'm glad I did, because my sister never picked up the violin after she quit, but I have enjoyed my piano ever since.

It's been like a friend over the years and, I'm a lousy pianist, but it's my psychiatrist. The piano is one of my favorite things.

Other things I enjoy around my home are some of these antiquities and mementoes, but they're not really important to me. Yet I've always loved Oriental art and I just picked up things as I went around. When I went to put those kimonos up on walls, my decorator said, "You don't want those things up." I said, "Listen, when my husband was living, I couldn't put them out, because he was so masculine. They were just too feminine for him. So I'm living here now and I'm putting my kimonos out, so if you don't like it, leave." She didn't leave. I wish she would have.

Believe it or not, I bought an elephant trunk at an antique store on Fifth Avenue. It took a year for the people to carve it.

Favorite pieces? Every one of them is a favorite piece, because I remember where I bought them and it's a wonderful memory of our travels together.

Art to me is memories. That's all. I don't buy art so that it will appreciate and I can get more for it. I buy art, because I like it and I keep it, because I like it. Each piece of art has a message to tell me. That's why I bought it. Chihuly, the glassmaker, created one of my pieces. I like it ,but although it's very expensive, I bought it for the memories.

I don't have a portrait of myself. That's not important to me. You can take a photograph. Never had a portrait painted and I don't want one painted. You could do a whole movie on me—I would rather have that. The portrait doesn't say a thing. It just shows a face.

Do I have a favorite song? I like and play *Claire De Lune*, but my favorite piece was *Stardust*. However, since my husband is gone, now it's *Unforgettable* sung by Nat King Cole. "Unforgettable, that's what you are … "

Now I'm going to tell you a story. Every couple years the symphony asks to use my home for Symphony Morning. It was an axillary of the symphony. All the women would come and we would give them a sweet tooth, coffee, and sweet rolls. We hosted 110 women between the dining room and the living room, while a four-piece quartet came in and entertained us. It was a blast. They sat in front of those windows in the living room where the curve is and they gave us a concert. Well, during that concert as the sun was setting, they started playing *Stardust*. When we looked outside with the sun going down, you could see little silver specks in the air. That was *Stardust*! You couldn't see it until the sun moved from one point to another and glittered on it. There was stardust outside when they played that song. Isn't that amazing?

Legend says that Hoagy Carmichael wrote that song as he sat in one of those boats on the Sarasota Bay. Maybe he saw that Stardust like I did.

The type of music I want playing when I go to the next place? Familiar music. I have danced to a lot of classical music.

I love *An American in Paris*, but *Rhapsody in Blue* is my favorite. When I hear the first note, the first four notes…D … M… G … C … A … B … C D BB BB … FA AEDB FA EFGC GABC FGAD EFG … I know the notes. Every one of them. From memory. Not with the chords, but just with one hand and one finger.

I love music.

When I hear the bells from the church ringing next door, I love that sound. A lot of people don't like that sound, but I do, except when I'm on the telephone.

It's a beautiful sound … church bells.

Chapter 22

A Good Party, Mahjong, & Bridge

"I don't throw a lot of parties. I find throwing parties a bit intimidating."

— Helen Mirren

I love parties.

I've thrown a lot of parties. I give a party for any big occasion in our lives. We've always had big parties. Amazingly many were on boats because when we lived in West Virginia, we lived on a river. We had a big paddle boat that could accommodate a couple hundred people who would dance as we floated down the river. Shoney's would cater our food, so we always had good food, with strawberry pies and Big Boys. We gave parties. We partied and we partied—wow!

It was like a scene from the movie *Showboat* on that paddleboat. You stood in the back and watched those paddles go round and round and make the boat move. It was wonderful. The paddleboat passed my house every day.

I've always loved water and lived on it or near it. I lived on the river in West Virginia and I lived on water when I was growing up. When I was at Crystal Lake, I was on water in the summertime. When I moved down to Florida, I lived both on

A Good Party, Mahjong, & Bridge

the Gulf of Mexico and on the bay in Sarasota.

For other parties, I rented out Sailor Circus in Sarasota, like I did for my husband's 75th birthday party. Alex was a clown and my granddaughter was a little girl, dressed up in a costume—we had a great party. We bought out the dress rehearsal the night before the show opened and we served the kids, the performers, the band, and our guests a barbecued dinner. Barbecue was going on outside of the tent. It was a great party! Some of those guests from New York had never been to a circus before, so they were amazed and enjoyed it tremendously.

I was definitely involved in planning the party. I even brought an act—some magicians from Las Vegas—to perform there. They were so marvelous. Alex and I had been in Vegas and seen them a couple months before and I asked my husband, "Could I go get them?" He thought it was a great idea. Alex even came in costume, let me tell you, he had a tough time getting into that clown outfit, because he had such a great big tutu and neck. (Laughs) He was so funny. He was a big clown. He liked the idea and was a good sport.

What makes a great party? The theme of the party. For our 50th Anniversary Party at the Hyatt, we had a reenactment of our wedding. My husband who'd been an All-American football player at Ohio State was in his old fashioned leather football helmet, with no face guard in front. When he played he lost six teeth in one football game when they kicked him in the side of his mouth and took six molars out. Anyway, we always had a theme for our parties. For most people, the 50th wedding anniversary is the one to celebrate if you're blessed to make it. For our 50th anniversary, we were blessed and made it. The rabbi performed our vows again and while it wasn't the same rabbi as our first wedding, it was a wonderful day and a great party. It was a big blow out. I'll tell you. We were remarried. I have pictures of my sister and me tap dancing.

For Alex's 80th birthday, we got Tommy Dorsey's band, which is now the Buddy Morrow band. I even had the woman, who was their singer, come back to sing. She was still their singer. It was wonderful.

Another party was our daughter's wedding dinner. The wedding was up in Clearwater at the Starlight Princess, which was over 100 years old. We all came down to Sarasota where we rented a boat, boarded it, and had dinner on the boat as it cruised up to the hotel. We gave everybody a captain's hat and we just had a wonderful time. It was a big wedding.

We gave great birthday parties. Fun parties. Mostly we had parties at the bowling alley, because we owned one. The kids loved it. We would put the bumpers up so that they could all get good scores. No one had gutter balls.

I have been involved in planning parties with organizations around town. When you are planning a party like this, you have to schedule a couple years ahead of time, especially in Sarasota where there are many organizations. You have to know the rules before you even begin to schedule a party. I get on committees for galas here, because I feel I can't help it.

Giving a good party? It's like with anything. You learn how to give a good one by doing it. After a while, you learn a lot.

I stopped giving my Ohio State party. It's been a while. I just can't wait on people like I once could.

Aside from parties, one of the things I also enjoyed was

A Good Party, Mahjong, & Bridge

Mahjong. I'll tell you why Mahjong is a wonderful game. When you make a mistake, you don't have a partner who yells at you like in Bridge, "Why did you need that card?"

I used to be a bridge player. When I had Emily I wanted to give her a childhood like my other children and I stopped going to bridge, so I could spend more time with my child. I'm glad I did. Because that's really the most important thing that you do in your life is raise a family.

I have played bridge since I was about ten years old, because my mother was an excellent bridge player and insisted that I learn how to play. But then we went from auction bridge to contract bridge. Well, that's a more difficult kind of bridge. At the time, Emily was a little girl, so I did not keep up with bridge. By that time Emily had grown up and I was done carpooling. Bridge had changed completely and it became very difficult. I didn't have time to learn bridge again, so I never went back to it. My mother was a very good bridge player and people would ask her to play at competitions at various places in Ohio. I played both bridge and Mahjong. Like I said, when you make a mistake in Mahjong no one gives you hell. When I make a mistake, I blame myself.

I've given so many parties. I don't think I can pick out one or remember all the parties I've given. One of my favorites was my 90th birthday party that we had at the University of Charleston. That was a favorite party. My children took care of all the details. Everything. They had shirts with my face painted on them. They had an ice carving of the Big Boy. They made the wrong ice carving, because they didn't make ice carvings in West Virginia. We had to go to Cincinnati. Well the Big Boy in Cincinnati isn't like Big Boy in Charleston. He doesn't hold up a hamburger with his hand. (Laughs) He's just a little figure running. When we took the covers off the Big Boy and realized it was an Ohio Big Boy and not a National Big Boy, we were so upset that it was stupid. But that was funny. My children did everything! They had little skits. The grandchildren talked about Grandma and my children talked about Momma and it was absolutely wonderful. It was at the University of Charleston where they have a huge ballroom. Right across the river from the ballroom is the capital of West Virginia with its beautifully lit up golden dome. It just was a glorious night. It was on the river, too. The river is between the capital and the university. During the day, we took a bus out and I showed them everything that I had done for the city of Charleston.

I still go to parties. I was at a party at Selby Gardens yesterday, sat there for a couple of hours, and look what it did to my hair. But it was a great party. Oh I love to party.

My favorite kind of party was one birthday party that we had. We owned a bowling alley and I had 88 people for my 88th birthday at the bowling alley. Most of my guests couldn't even lift a ball. So we put up the little bumpers, so they wouldn't get any gutter balls and they all got good scores. We had more fun. We served them and we had a wonderful time. Joann planned it and when she plans a party. WOW!

Joann is the one who will plan my 100th Birthday.

We could have it at the Municipal Auditorium, because I know so many people.

But, God only knows.

Chapter 23

Health and Growing Old

"Old age ain't no place for sissies."

— Bette Davis

I have been relatively healthy my whole life.

However, I do have Sjogren's syndrome, which I've had since I was 52. It's an autoimmune disease where you become dehydrated. When my doctor was examining my eyes and I didn't tear up, he said, "Have you ever been examined for Sjogren's syndrome?" I said, "What's Sjogren's syndrome?" He explained, "It's a disease that's been known about for maybe 50 years and many people don't realize they have it. It's the drying out of your system where your glands shut down." I said, "Oh my God. How would you know? You're here to examine my teeth." He said, "Well, you've told me the history of your teeth. That you always had to go to the dentist." My mother always told me that I hope the man you marry sets up an endowment for your teeth, because my teeth were expensive. By the time I was 52 years old, I had every tooth in my mouth capped. They decayed rapidly even with the best dental care that you could have. After meals I had to brush my teeth. My mother made me, because my bills were expensive and she didn't want to pay them. She insisted on me taking good care of my teeth. Anyway, the dentist said, "Go to a doctor and get diagnosed."

I went to the doctor and sure enough discovered that I had Sjogren's syndrome. The first thing that shut down was my salivary glands. I have no saliva. Because I have no saliva to take the bacteria out, any bacteria that I have lodged in there decayed my teeth. I'm a very slow eater, because I'm dry here when I swallow. I'm still slow.

Looking into the future and my 100th birthday party, I'm afraid I'm not going to able to make it because of Sjogren's syndrome. They have a foundation. I wrote to them and they told me everything that's going to happen to me and I can't do anything about it. There's no pills. No medicine. No exercise. It's a drying up of your whole body. It has started already. I'm going to the Lighthouse so I can read my newspaper in the morning. My eyes are going. Nothing I can do. Four million people have it in the United States. It's an autoimmune disease. My lacrimal and salivary glands are gone. My ears need hearing aids and my eyes are going. My skin is going. Look at my skin. It's tissue paper. My hydrating glands are gone. I don't have any hydration.

I'm doing the best I can and doing better than most people.

The next thing to go were my eyes. I have macular degeneration, because of my dryness. For most of life, I had good eyesight and didn't need glasses until I was 52. It has come back. It left for a while, but I had these two glands that didn't work—because they don't come back. Once your glands are gone, they're gone. My macular degeneration problem is also getting worse and worse, but that didn't bother me until I turned 95.

You see, my skin it's like tissue paper. There's no moisture under it. I have to grease myself like a pig all the time. I say you're ready to put me on the spit. It's not funny. I itch all the time. It was so bad that I went to my son-in-law who is a dermatologist and he couldn't fix it. I fixed it. I took Aveeno that comes in a tube and mixed in three table spoons of grape seed oil in that tube of Aveeno and applied it.

Overall, I have had wonderful health. My mom and dad were pretty healthy until later in life. What they died from wouldn't have killed them today. My dad died from taking too many aspirins. He took 40 of them a day! Forty a day to fight off the pain caused from his horrible arthritis. My mother died from cancer of the kidney, which spread from the bowel, because she never went to a doctor about her condition.

I attribute my good health to my diet. My father was in the chicken business—butter, eggs, and poultry wholesale. We had chicken six days a week and meat on Friday night—a brisket for the Sabbath. Our chickens were range-fed. There were no hatcheries back then, because they had not been invented yet. I attribute our good health to that, because my sister lived to 92, my brother lived to 90, and my other brother is now 94, and I'm 99.

When I wake up, I'm not pain free. I'm so dry that I can't stand it. I get up at night and drink water, but I sleep so good, that when I go back to bed, in two minutes I'm fast asleep. Sleeping well is such a gift. Oh, my God, yes. My daddy slept well. I guess I just inherited it.

I don't have to block things out from the day, because I have a prayer and mention every member of my immediate family in the prayer. I talk to God and thank God for this beautiful world he gave us to live in. I pray to God that hate will go out of this world. I pray to God to wrap his arms around the world and give it love every night. If I fall asleep in the middle of my prayers, because that's how easy I go to sleep, I wake up in the middle of the night and finish my prayers. I know just where I left off.

Regarding my diet, every morning I have a peanut butter sandwich on bread from Oregon with a pound of raisins in each loaf. It's a darker, heavier bread, 200 calories to a slice. Then I put three tablespoons full of natural ground organic peanut butter on it. Being that I have difficulty with my teeth, I drink a glass of organic apple juice. For lunch, I usually have soup and half a sandwich. And I love fish. I adore fish. I eat very little red meat, maybe once a week.

Regarding exercise, well, I guess for the first 15 years of my young life, I studied ballet almost every day. I was always tall and thin. My father was tall—about 6'1"—my mother was tall at about 5'7."

My advice to my grandchildren about leading a healthy life?

Don't smoke. I took drags from my date's cigarettes when I was young. (Laughs) Everybody smoked then. You wanted to be a part of the crowd, so you would take a drag. Definitely get involved in some sort of athletics. I played basketball and tennis. I thought golf was stupid, because why should you get mad when you can't hit the ball right? I decided, "Why should I be angry at myself all the time, so I'm not getting involved." But I did like tennis.

When I was young, I drank Cuba libres, but as I've gotten older, I seem to be intolerant to liquor. Now I drink maybe once a month—a vodka with cranberry juice and very little vodka. I'm allergic to wine—it puts me to sleep. Three sips of wine and I could have my head down in my plate sleeping.

Getting older, it's the greatest feeling in the world, but you have to start coping with the physical things that happen to you. But you cope with them. You can't beat them. I mean your body is wearing out. Just cope and keep going. Don't stop. Because when you stop, you're never able to get out of bed.

I'm not a big complainer, but I complain sometimes. I complain about how confining it is when you aren't well. When people ask me how I feel, I say "with my hands."

Let's face it, as we get older—if we are blessed to grow older—we start falling apart.

As I told you, I was diagnosed with Sjogren's syndrome, when I was 52 and it came back when I was 95, which is very unusual. From 95 to 98 I had a lot of things happen that could have happened much earlier. God has been so very good to me.

When I say coping—I mean you have to adjust—there is nothing that you can do about it. Attitude is everything. I push myself sometimes. Sometimes I feel like not doing a thing and I go ahead and do what I'm supposed to do. When I come home, I congratulate myself on going.

I set goals for myself. Sometimes by evening, I'm tired and I can't physically go to the event. Sometimes when I don't have an ache or pain, I say to myself, "WOW, isn't this wonderful." Like right now. As I'm sitting here, I don't have an ache or a pain.

I like what Bette Davis said "Growing old isn't for sissies." My line is, "You have to be brave to grow old." I have two PhDs and I can't heal a thing—but I'm a doctor twice. (Laughs)

Some days, I don't have a lot of things planned. Today I have an interview. The next thing that I have to do is go out to Lighthouse for the Blind and get something to help me read the newspaper. I can't do my puzzles in the morning, because I can't read them anymore. I can't find a pair of glasses that help me very much. That's a big thing in my life. That's the first time in my life that I have ever had to get help for my sight. It's not only to help me do my crossword puzzles, but I can't read the articles in the paper either without straining my eyes. It helps me read letters and anything else. After that, it's an unusual day, because I don't have any place that I have to go for lunch. (Laughs) I've been trying to take a shower now for three days. So I'm going to take a shower next! (Laughs) Then this evening, I'm going to a book signing of a friend of mine. Afterward there is a party, but I'm not going to the party, because they are younger and they don't dance the way I used to dance. I can't dance anymore, because of my legs, so I'm coming home.

How did I get to be almost 100?

I was on a monkey diet. I picked the monkeys, because they are the smartest animals. I start each of my days off with my monkey breakfast—two pieces of raisin bread, three tablespoons of organic peanut butter, and a banana with glass of apple juice, because an apple a day keeps the doctor away.

Today I have no lunch plans. When I go to lunch, I like to go to the Bijou and various places around town.

Back in the day, Shoney's had a salad bar with entrees on it too, but mostly salad items on it. I stayed healthy, because I ate the salad bar at Shoney's.

A lot of times, the luncheons that I attend are for organizations that I support in town. If I like the cause and I can't go to the luncheon, I send money, because I believe very strongly in what they are doing.

Sometimes I overdo it. I did yesterday.

Am I afraid of slowing down? My friends are slowing down. But most of my friends are gone. Even if I wanted to slow down, I would hate to quit all those things that I'm in.

I've been in good health all my life and I've been grateful. Oh, my God. Imagine. No headaches! I had one headache, a migraine, when I was up in a plane back in the 1950s, when we went from Chicago to California. On our approach to Big Sur, we came down very rapidly and we were not pressurized well enough for me to take the descent. On the way to the hotel, I got this violent headache. I never had one before. At the hotel, I lay in the bed and told everybody to get out of the room.

"I don't want anybody around. I don't want any noise. I just want to lay here."

It was horrible. I went to sleep and finally in the morning when I woke up, it was gone.

But that's not bad though—one headache in nearly 100 years.

I can thank God for that and everything else.

Part Five

REFLECTIONS ON THINGS THAT MATTER

Chapter 24

Israel

"Above all, this country is our own. Nobody has to get up in the morning and worry what his neighbors think of him. Being a Jew is no problem here."

— Golda Meir

Routine has always been a part of the Betty's life. Things that she does each and every day set her schedule and attitude in the right direction. Reading the paper and staying informed is something she treasures and values, but something that's harder to do as her eyes begin to lose their strength. But make no mistake, Betty can still see and feel the world around her—she is still an integral part of it. Sure, she may struggle with focus as she solves her daily crossword puzzles, but she plods through—a believer in the doing. Staying involved with the many organizations that she gives to generously, helping others get involved in the business of giving while they are living. That's just two more components of her routine. Helping people, many people with a scholarship here, an endowment there, or merely a heartfelt hug that someone really needed—all part of a wonderful daily routine. As days wind down, a big part of her heart looks back and counts the blessings that the good Lord has blessed her with for her long and beautiful life.

At night, she says her prayers—going through a massive list, praying for the well-being of her large family, endless numbers of friends, and for the overall condition of the planet and the people who inhabit it. Once again, part of her routine—Betty's routine. Thanking God for everything. Every day. And sometimes in the midst of the prayers, when she falls asleep and then awakens like a fine-tuned clock or a well-run Ohio State offense, picks up the prayers just where she left off. It is a routine that she lives by. Betty is an All-American girl when it comes to giving and living each and every one of her days with purpose, passion, and a routine that is anything but routine.

Her days now are not and never have been filled with mailing it in. She is engaged. And with every day she's blessed to have is filled with the doing of big things that in the end she hopes will make the world a better and more loving place.

As she counts her blessings, makes her appointments, and says her prayers, she is still concerned. She still wants to make a difference in the lives of so many. She is still, more than ever concerned with issues of homelessness, educating children, and of course the future of Israel. And of course she wants to see to it that her family knows what's important in life. That's the purpose of this memoir—to leave something behind that her family will pick up from time to time and say, "That's how Grandma did it." Or "That's what she thought deep in her heart."

Israel

As she approaches and passes the century mark, there are still so many causes that ignite her into action to open up her big heart and help capture her heart.

But at the top of the list, as she goes through her daily routine, at the very top of the list, on an even higher shelf than her philanthropy, is her love and appreciation for her big and wonderful family.

Betty is grateful for that more than anything—her family. Children. Grandchildren. Great-grandchildren. In-laws who are as close as her kids. Everyone in her big family. Those that are still here. And those that have moved on to a better place. As she goes through her routine, she remembers and is grateful for them all, as she remembers them all in her prayers—part of her daily routine.

For now though, she wakes up, has her juice, and fills out the crossword puzzle. With that fabulous smile, she fills out the six-letter word for the country in the Middle East that gained its independence in 1948.

If these other countries would just leave Israel alone. It's less than 100 years old. Israel celebrates its 70th birthday in 2018. It went from barren land to a paradise. It was a calling for me. Israel is the only place where the Jews are free in the world—a place where Jews would not be bothered all the time. They needed a homeland. Someplace in the world. They couldn't come to the United States, because they had a quota on Jews.

I started becoming more active in philanthropic endeavors with Israel when I joined Hadassah, which was the first unit to go over there to actually help improve the land. They sent nurses over there, who found that the sanitation was horrible. They had open ditches. The first thing they did was put pipes in to carry sewage away. They tried to save every drop of water that fell. They planted trees. It's very heavily forested now, but they didn't have those forests 69 years ago. They would start with a little tree about a foot tall. Then they would put a long hose directly to the roots of the tree so that nothing would be wasted along the way. When the water went through the hose, each tree got water, but nothing in between the trees got water. They built forests, which changed the climate over Israel, because trees naturally affect our ozone. Everything Hadassah did was for Israel and the people.

I first visited Israel in 1946 before it became a nation. The feeling I got when I went there? Honestly I thought, "What are the Jews going to do with this country? It's just nothing but desert." That's what it was. They had cities—different meccas where people went to trade and sell their wares. Actually, Jerusalem was the only big city, because it had been there for 3,000 years.

Alex and I went over that year as a group with the United Jewish Appeal from the United States. Our problem or challenge was: "How can we make this a homeland?" I was very hopeful at that time, because that's where a lot of Jewish people lived. These very amiable people were thrilled that we had come there, because they needed help from not only Jews in the United States, but from all over the world, who had raised a lot of money for Israel. It was the only place where Jews from Europe could go and feel safe.

Israel

We went back to America to discuss what else we could do for Israel and we have been involved ever since. Alex had been the head of fundraising for the whole state of West Virginia, but there were not very many Jewish people living there. He was in the forefront, where I was not as much out front, as those were my child-bearing years.

We knew how important it was to help Israel. What would you do for people who had been incarcerated, survived, and wanted to go to a place where they wouldn't be exterminated?

We really didn't hear about the Holocaust until the war was over. Remember, we didn't have television and the instantaneous communication that we have now. Today you get information in one minute. You couldn't do that back then. To think that they killed six million people who had no defense at all. No defense. In concentration camps, you have no arms or anything to defend yourself. Children were separated from parents and husbands from wives. It was worse than slavery, because at least with slavery you stayed alive. In Germany, the Jews were murdered. Oh, my God. The sense of evil still shocks me. I can't go through the Holocaust Museum, because it doesn't hurt my heart—it hurts my soul. It's one of the reasons I've never taken a complete tour of the Holocaust Museum, because the horrors were so terrible then.

People were inhumane. These same men would come home and sit down with their families and children at night and eat their dinners, after having done their evil acts during the day. Think of that. After killing children and babies at work, they would sit down with their children. They took babies. What did a baby ever do wrong?

Still even today, some people claim that the Holocaust didn't happen.

There aren't many survivors left. Our survivors, the last few are now in the late eighties and nineties and they will all be gone soon. Regarding the deniers, they are just people who don't like the Jews and want to portray Jews as being bad people.

Israel is still targeted today. They have no defense. Their enemies want to kill them, because they are in the way. The heart has gone out of the world.

I've been a big a proponent of education and have been involved in helping Israel in that way as well. You have to help. Who in the world is going to help Israel? Only the Jews help the Jews.

We gave to the general fund. My husband led the effort for many years. When they started doing Project Renewal, which was supposed to renew a town, our town was Tel Mond. My husband helped build a library there and it's turned into a community center and a bigger library, simply because the high schools there closed the libraries. I've been told that people go to our library, because it was better funded. It's gotten to be a famous place. When we first got involved, there were Moroccan Jews living there. It's developed. It's supposed to be a wonderful place to live, with homes ranging from $500,000 to a million dollars, and a place to go to, if you want to live in a nice town.

We also built a school in Israel—Kiryat Yam. I'm crazy about sports, having had a husband who was involved in sports. When I went to see the last Olympics a few years ago,

Israel

I realized that there were three Kenyans who ran around the oval carrying their flag of Kenya. I decided, "We've got Ethiopian Jews in Israel. Why not develop their talents?"

Ethiopians won, because they were raised on a higher elevation in the desert. The Jews in Ethiopia were farmers who farmed high above the desert, because you can't farm in the desert. They had no education and no schools in Ethiopia for children. So I thought, I'll develop their talents. I knew there were Ethiopians in Kiryat Yam, a city near Haifa, on the Mediterranean on the bay of Haifa.

I thought, wow! The same area that I was going to help develop, 20% of the population were Ethiopians and 20% Russian immigrants, both first-generation. Their parents were immigrants. The other 60% of the town were Israelis. It was a middle to lower class town, because there were so many immigrants. I thought that I would elevate the town standing. When I went over there, the Russian and Ethiopian immigrants didn't talk to each other, because the Russians felt superior. When they played soccer, they played against each other. Well I said, "That's wrong. They should play with each other."

So I put in a soccer stadium with grandstands and an Olympic track around the whole thing. I even put the same surface that they ran on in the Olympics. It cost me a lot of money, but I wanted to go first class. First class.

We built a running track, because my Ethiopians were from high elevations in Africa. They were farmers and didn't live in the desert. I was hoping someday that we would have Olympic medal winners from Ethiopia. I pictured seeing them running

The Joy of Giving is the Joy of Living

to victory while carrying a flag from Israel around the stadium. That would be the greatest joy to see that.

Then I gave money for a soccer field, because the Russian Jews, first-generation in Israel, didn't get along with the Ethiopian Jews. That was a normal thing because Ethiopian Jews had no education when they arrived in Israel. It took a while for them to catch up.

We continued to build there and I helped fund a science center, an Ethiopian center for the Ethiopians, a beautiful building with a museum, and finally a library where they can use a computer 24-hours a day.

The high school was built in 1946 before Israel was even a nation. They had no air conditioning, no bomb shelter, and no electricity of any kind. They had sockets in the wall, but no electric equipment of today that they could use for teaching. We did everything but knock the school down. The brick walls remained, but had been painted, but now the paint had fallen off. I remodeled the whole building and we removed all the doors and windows. They put royal blue windows in with royal blue doors. We took the steps, railings, floors, and lockers and we redid every classroom electronically, so they could use their laptops. We put Skype in quite a few classrooms.

Eventually my new high school in Kiryat Yam was awarded the best in the state of Israel. In five years, it has gone from 41% to 91% matriculation rate. It is run by ORT. Forty per cent of the students in that school are either Ethiopian or Russian Jews and they get along.

Recently we got an accommodation from the Secretary

of Education from Israel that my school was number one in the state of Israel.

Technion, the best and highly acclaimed technical school in Israel and one of the best in the world, who have produced a number of Nobel Prize winners, came over and was teaching in my school.

That makes me so happy that I could burst, absolutely burst. So my friends gave me wet suit so that I wouldn't burst. They loved me and they didn't want me to burst. (Laughs) I'm doing jokes now. I like humor.

It's been a while since I have been to Israel. The last time I was there for the dedication. It's been years. It's a long ride on a plane—13 hours. And now I'm 99. The family foundation did it, so my whole family was with me. All my children and their spouses.

How did it feel? The most wonderful feeling in the world. Here I was in Israel where my grandmother always wanted to be buried. I did all this and all I could think of was how proud my grandmother would have been of me—Grandma Goldman who was saving money to buy land in Israel when I was a little girl.

That's full circle. (Emotional) It's wonderful that I could do that. I believe that she's watching and guiding my hand, and if she's not watching, her wonderful spirit is within me and has been a big part of my life. She's made me aware of being a Jew and helping my fellow man.

The makeup of the students who are attending Kiryat Yam, the children that are there, their parents immigrated into the port of Kiryat Yam. They landed there and stayed, because they have no money to go anywhere else.

It is one of the accomplishments I'm most proud of, along with the Glasser-Schoenbaum Center here in Sarasota; the innovative childhood training school in Columbus, Ohio, and the wonderful non-profit complex in Charleston, West Virginia.

The theme of helping with education and my mantra, "To give to live," is the only way we can overcome and prevent another Holocaust or the terror prevalent in our world. The only way forward is for people around the world to start liking the Jews and see what they have done in this world instead of disliking them.

I worry about Israel today in my 99th year, for sure, because they're still discriminated against. How does this get resolved? That's a great question.

I think that what's happened is that love has gotten out of the world and hatred has taken its place. Hatred goes right to the Republican and Democrats in our country. The Republicans hate the Democrats. And the Democrats hate the Republicans. They won't sit down and talk it out and see what they are doing to this country. They're slicing this country in half and they're both wrong. Our constitution says it all, "Of the people, by the people and for the people." This is not for the Republicans, by the Republican or for the Democrats, by the Democrats. In this election, I think the most important issues are foreign affairs. With the Iran developing the bomb and with Syria taking over all this land, the world is the most important thing.

Iran has recently signed their bombs in Hebrew,

Israel

"DESTROY ISRAEL." That is my number one concern. One of those bombs will destroy the whole state of Israel. Wipe Israel off the map. Would that scare you? To me that's a modern day Holocaust.

That's the end of the world we know. Because everybody would be mad at Iran—because they started it. I'll tell you about that bomb. We have a bomb, too. We have never threatened anybody with our bomb, but the minute that their bomb goes off, the second that bomb goes off, honey, our bomb will go off, because we'll know it. We'll punch a button and one will go to Iran. So how does that help Israel when it's bombed off the map?

What do I think is going to happen to the world?

At the rate we're going, there's going to be a third World War. There's not going to be a world left, once they have that bomb.

Mohammed gave them a way of religion. He talks that Palestine is theirs. In the whole Koran, it does not mention Palestine once. How could he honestly say that Palestine belongs to the Arabs, if in the time that the Muslim religion was created, he never went to Palestine? It's not mentioned in the Koran once.

The Fundamentalists live very well and very happily in their countries. The Arab radicals will not sit down with Jews. And while it's a small percentage of maybe under 10 % that are radical Arabs, you don't need many radicals to do damage. You just need one bomb.

The development at Kiryat Yam is a lot more than the school. I put in a sea aquarium that's in Kiryat Yam. It's a small one, but you think you're under water and all around you, so you see what's under the sea. Then we put in our planetarium and a school there. It's run by the man who is the only medal winner in the state of Israel. I'm ashamed that we only have one medal. It's for windsurfing. The winner is the head of our aquatic center.

We also put in a large cultural center. A woman from Sarasota, Florida, built the auditorium in the school. A multitude of events are held at our cultural center and not just for those in the school. The cultural center is for the Ethiopians, where we have a room that has 24 computers. In Ethiopia, they had no education. They seek those computers, because now they know Hebrew and can use the computers. They're curious about the world. Things that we learned early on, they're now learning off the computers. They adore education. They sign up for an hour and they will get up at 2 o'clock in the morning to get their hour in, so that they can get an education.

Their cultural center has a synagogue in it like you would have in Ethiopia—a mud building with a thatched roof and a dirt floor. They were very religious in Ethiopia in the jungle. They had their Torah; their services, their Sabbath, and they wouldn't do anything on the Sabbath. The only thing they had was their religion. They were very observant. The rabbi was so holy, you couldn't touch him. You spoke to him, but you could not touch him. He was untouchable. They respected their religion. It was beautiful to see that all these thousands of years of living in the jungle that they have preserved their religion.

Israel

That place also had a museum for the Ethiopians and a library by the Ethiopian center. It's very large complex, but centrally located.

In essence, we have created this place where two groups of people who didn't get along—get along. That's quite a model for the world. I attribute that to them finding out they are all Jews and they want the same thing. They want peace.

That is what the Jews of the world want—PEACE. If the Jews could only live in peace, we'd have a lot of wonderful things happening in this world. Right now, they have something that is helping Lou Gehrig's disease and they say it's working. At the Hadassah Hospital in Israel is where they are doing the research. It's absolutely working and has stopped the disease in some people. In other people, they are better. So many things have been discovered at Technion. Stem cell research almost originated in Israel at Technion.

Still there is so much anti-Semitism in the world. How the Jews of the world want to be treated is simple. Our motto is, "T I KKUN OLAM." It means to heal the world. To heal the world, it doesn't mean just Jews. To heal all the world. This is what we hope for—that love pervades the world, instead of hatred. And accepting people as Jews is part of that.

Right now, it's horrible. There's anti-Semitism all over this world. Some countries say they have banned it and that it will never happen again. But when countries have trouble internally, they blame it on the Jews.

Shockingly it's happening right now on some American college campuses, regarding Israel and anti-Semitism. It's difficult to combat, because some of these groups hide behind protection afforded them by their First Amendment rights of Freedom of Speech.

I have one question. Why do they have rights, but we don't have the rights? They don't let us have the rights. They boycott us and make fun of us. Of course, there is a lot more of them than of us. The universities are allowing it. The administration slaps their hands, but they don't do anything about it. We (Israel) are discriminated against.

Some have said the solution is to create your own videos, but where are you going to play those videos? The people who don't like us won't play them and the people who like us already know our situation.

Without the Jews, there would be no Hollywood. Old Hollywood. Classic Hollywood. But today's Hollywood is different and seems not to speak up on Israel's behalf. They've gotten blasé. They're Americanized and it doesn't seem to bother the Jews. They didn't go through the Holocaust. I didn't go through it or know about the Holocaust until the war started. We didn't know they were killing all those Jews over there. The news never went out. We didn't have television until the late 40s. When all this was happening in Germany, we didn't have people from the newspapers going over there to see what's happening over there and reporting it back to us. It just went on without us knowing in the United States.

People should know what's happening now. But they don't know. They are denying it happened. Even with all our technology, we see these things happening in real time—for instance, ISIS killing Jews, Christians, and Muslims. Today's Holocaust is being broadcast in living color. They're killing non-Jews. The Muslims are killing their own people—already 300,000 people in Syria have been killed.

I am saddened as the world watches this take place today. Mothers who allow their children to be trained to take explosives and go kill themselves for a cause—that's a sick mother. That's inhumane. They teach them to hate. And you know what? They don't allow education for everybody, because they are afraid that the children will become smarter than they are. And they don't want that. They want to be the dominant one in their family.

Chapter 25

Grandma Goldman

"No one has ever become poor by giving."

— Anne Frank

We were brought up as reformed Jews.

I'm sorry for that, because I believe more in the tradition than the tradition I got. You must remember we were the first generation of Jews in this country. My grandparents wanted to be American Jews, instead of Jewish Americans, so they put American first.

My grandmother was a rabbi's child and she was religious her whole life. Her name was Fanny Goldman. She was my favorite grandmother. From Grandma Goldman I learned to give. She taught me the gift of giving and she was so poor. Her husband was killed when he was 32-years old. She was left in this country with two boys and a daughter and a baby on the way. They lived in Kentucky. He was a trainer for a big horse farm. He was taking money from the race track to the bank and he was held up and killed. After that, she had to live at her brothers in the basement of his home in Cincinnati, Ohio, and raise her four children. She was remarried to a fine man and she had a decent life, but was poor.

She taught me about giving.

Every Friday night, she put money in three little tin boxes on her stove. I kept saying to her, "Grandma, what do you do with all that money?" To me I was a little girl just five years old and I wondered what she did with all that money that she put in there. Nickels and dimes. I remember what she said, "I'm saving money to buy land in (Palestine) Israel. When I die I want to have a bag of sand from Israel and they're going to lay it under my head so that I can die with the sand of Israel under my head."

It wasn't Israel then, it was Palestine. Back then, my grandmother said, "She was buying the land in Israel." Now today, Palestine says we took the land.

That's where I started thinking about what she did and it influenced my life. She was so religious that she went over and lived behind the Synagogue. Every day they had prayer meetings. The men had prayer meetings in the morning at that time. She would go over in the hall, but they wouldn't let her in. No women were allowed. Praying is called davening—that's the Jewish word for prayer. She would daven out in the hall twice a day every day of her life. In the rain, in the snow she would go over to the Synagogue and pray. She was beautiful. Beautiful. Beautiful. She knew Hebrew because her father, a rabbi taught her. At that time girls didn't study the bible.

She's the one who took care of us during the summers at the lake. Grandma Goldman. What an angel. What an angel. She taught me the gift of giving. Her whole life.

When she planted something in the garden, I saw it grow so wonderful and productive.

My mother let us hang stockings until we knew there was no Santa Claus. And that was the end of that. We always knew from other kids that there was no Santa Claus. You wanted to believe it, because it was a nice holiday. We'd hang up our stockings and in the morning we'd open up our gifts. We did that for quite a few years.

We celebrated Hanukkah and Yom Kippur. We celebrated them all. But we weren't as religious as we should have been, because we were reformed.

Grandma Goldman was kind of the glue that helped us stick to some of our traditions. She reminded us of our traditions and we'd go over there and light the candles with her. I don't remember celebrating any holidays with my other grandmother, who also lived in Dayton. Grandma Goldman was my grandmother on my mother's side and Grandma Frank was grandmother on my father's side.

Both my grandmothers were of Jewish decent. 100 per cent. A thousand percent. When we visited Grandma Frank, we had to take our shoes off and walk on newspapers and sit in the kitchen. She'd give us each a cookie and a glass of milk and we were supposed to sit there and not open our mouths.

My wonderful grandmother's tombstone is in Dayton, Ohio—Fanny Goldman (1870-1945). I think of the big footprint that she left. Oh how she would have loved to have known about this. Oh, my God. Oh, my God.

I can still see that kitchen. Yes I can and I can see her putting those coins into those tin boxes. It was a small kitchen with a coal stove. She had a nice house. And the three containers were on a shelf on top of the stove. I was five years old. I was never knee high to a grasshopper—I was never knee high. I was always tall and skinny.

She never did go to Israel. She was never well to do enough to go there and make the trip. When her husband was murdered, she was 29 years old. She'd only been here for three years when that happened and she ended up raising four children. She survived and went out and got a job making cigar boxes in Cincinnati, Ohio. She worked in a factory. She lived in her brother's basement and they looked after each other.

Where the Palestinians said that we stole their land, I know we didn't. Not only that, there was a Blue Box Program with Hadassah and whenever we had a mitzvah, something wonderful happened in our lives. We put money in the blue box and when they came to collect the boxes, mine always ran over, because there were so many beautiful things that happened in my life. I remember putting money in the blue boxes to buy land in Israel. It was always to buy it. It was never to steal it.

But it all started because of Grandma Goldman. She is the sweet woman who taught me the joy of giving.

If I could talk to her right now as if she were here, I would say, "Grandma, you taught me the most wonderful lesson of life. No matter how much you have, you should give—even if its pennies. Those pennies bought land in Israel."

Chapter 26

Joy of Giving/Joy of Living

"Real generosity toward the future lies in giving all to the present."

— Albert Camus

I can't say it enough times, but the person who really influenced my giving was my poor grandma, Grandma Goldman.

What a beautiful lady, just beautiful. She was my biggest influence and got me when I was five years old. She taught me about giving. The most beautiful woman I've ever known in my life. And my mother, her daughter, is next.

I didn't think of her every day, but I think of her often. I have so many people to think of, with all my children, grandchildren, and great-grandchildren. If I thought of them every day, I wouldn't get anything done. I remember them all in my prayers.

She's the last one I remember in my prayers when I talk to God. I know she's up there with God. I know she is. She taught me that no matter how poor you are, if you give, you get a wonderful feeling from it. She sacrificed. She truly sacrificed things so that she could give.

As far as any mentors who influenced my giving, I didn't have any, because whatever organization I joined, I usually was the biggest giver, so I didn't need a mentor to tell me to give. Now Alex, he was a very giving soul. He was amazing.

There are givers and takers and I've always been in the giving camp. I've never been a taker, ever. Thank God, I didn't have to be a taker. Some people are in positions where they have to be takers and they can't help it. They have little hope.

Alex and I were in the same camp and on the same page. I never resented any money he gave away, ever. I never really gave away money until my husband passed away. Oh I would give $5,000 here and $5,000 there, but I never gave away a million dollars like my husband was doing. I let him have the pleasure of doing it. He made it, so he could give it away.

What do I think that Alex would say about the philanthropy I'm involved with today? Every time I do something, I look up to heaven and I say, "I did good, Alex. Didn't I?" I always want to be sure that he would be giving to the same things that I'm giving to today. And I feel good about that.

Alex even gave to women's organizations like the Women's Resource Center. I've been on the board ever since he passed away.

I think I've had some influence on people giving and I'm proud of that. Many people come up to me and say they were inspired by what I said in a speech that I've given about giving.

Barbara Brizdle was the head of the JFCS and she came up to me not long ago and said, "I always gave and I gave good. But now I really give."

Another individual I influenced is Ernie Kretzmer. Ernie was standing right here in this living room about 20 years ago when I hosted big gifts dinner for the United Jewish Appeal. At the time, "He gave very nicely." So after the dinner, I started talking to him and I said, "Ernie, I know you have a lot of money and you're getting older. I just wondered, because I'm worried about what to do with my money when I die. What are you going to do with yours when you die?" He said, "I'm giving it all away." I said, "Why wait to give it all away? You won't know if they will spend it on what you left the money for."

If you give it to the temple to have a Sunday school party in perpetuity, and heavy rains are coming in, they won't have the party—they'll fix the roof. So why don't you give it away right now. So Ernie started giving and he gave a million dollars to the ballet to build a building to house their dancers. Now every time he sees me, he comes up and hugs me so hard that he almost knocks me down. (Laughs) He tells everyone, "Betty Schoenbaum has been my mentor for giving."

I am overwhelmed that I have influenced people that way. You know I didn't do this until recently, when my husband passed away 21 years ago.

Another person, Lee Wetherington, a prominent builder in Sarasota, has spoken about how I've influenced his giving. He heard me give an acceptance speech after I received an award on why I give. The following week, Lee gave one million dollars to the Boys and Girls Club.

My motto or slogan in life is:

The joy of giving is the joy of living.

I get wonderful feelings from giving. One day, I saw a student of mine at Ringling College, to whom I gave a scholarship to at a little luncheon before she started school. She was from South Charleston, West Virginia, and I told her, "I'm so glad that you're my student, being that you're from West Virginia.

Well this young woman, who was a shy little Korean girl, was part of the team that won the animation award at Ringling. She was part of the making of "The Hero," which won the Academy Award for an animated movie.

The stage was crowded with lots of people, but I noticed my girl, Sarah Schabach, receiving her award. *Wow!* I thought, *Oh, my God. Imagine that. She got there in June and the following March she's got her Oscar.* I called her to congratulate her. She's now in charge of lighting and doing quite well. She met a Jewish boy in school and they were married in December.

I have books that contain all the letters from students that we've provided scholarships. There are at least ten of these books and they are filled with thousands of letters. It's not only what the letters mean to me, but what those students have become.

One book contains letters from West Virginia I received since 1989. Those are scholarships that I've given. These are all students that received scholarships from my endowment from the West Virginia University for students who cannot afford to go to school. I give them five years of college. They borrow the money from my fund to go to school. I pay the room, books, and tuition. I do not pay for board simply because when my husband went to school, he played football and was a waiter at his fraternity house and made money, because he needed it for spending money. Alex learned how to handle money during his days in college, so I figured I'd do the same with these students. They work 20 hours a week and at that time, the wage was $5.00 an hour. You had $100 to take care of all of your incidentals when I started this back in 1989. So they had plenty of money to spend on themselves. If they wanted to take a date out, they could.

We loaned the money to them for five years. For every year that they remained in West Virginia and taught, they had to maintain a B average. If they fell below a B average, they lost their scholarship. They were all A and B students the whole time. If they stayed in West Virginia for five years, they would have no college loan at all and not owe anything for their education.

People have asked me, "What does that mean to you?"

What does it mean? How would you all feel, if you sent thousands of children to college? I've done thousands already. This isn't my only college. These are the ones that are closest to my heart—the one in West Virginia and, of course, the one in Ohio. I was born and brought up in Ohio and we lived in Ohio. This book (points to letters) is from the scholarships I gave in West Virginia. I am bursting with joy.

Sometimes they feel like my children. But there are so many. I'm not in West Virginia anymore. I don't keep in close touch like I used to. I would go up there every year and we would have a reunion. Before a football game, we would have a breakfast and all the women would come in and see me. It was absolutely a joy to find out where these people were and how they got there. About twenty or thirty of the ones who lived in that area would come and be with me. I have a scrapbook in there of the people hugging me. See—I was already a hugger. (Laughs)

I have to tell you about the Milken Foundation. Each year, this foundation gives away two and half million dollars for awards to the two best teachers in each state. They give 100 awards away—two and half million dollars with $25,000 going to each teacher One of my students received this award twice—the only one who ever received the award twice! He got it ten years ago and he got it again last year.

I read each one of these letters. Every one of them. When I receive it—I read it. Assigning my assistant, Ray, to read them wouldn't give me a thrill. I want the thrill.

It's one of the important things about my legacy. When I give funds to people—Number one, I hope that they get a good education. Secondly, I hope that it gives them a way to make a living throughout their lives. It's just a wonderful feeling you get from helping people. They always write me letters. Some send me pictures of their family. Some write me when they buy a new house and they give me a picture of it. I appreciate that, because most people don't write letters anymore. No one has ever thanked me by email. You won't find an email in there. Many of the people hand write their letters with beautiful script, when they don't have a typewriter or computer. Letter writing—that's a beautiful lost art—the thank you note. And I'm still getting them. They are still sending them to me. Every year.

I don't feel gratitude that I could do it—I feel blessed that I could do it. I don't give back—I give to the future. Of the letters I receive, the ones from West Virginia are the warmest.

I'm blessed that Grandma Goldman gave me this gene, this giving gene.

I don't give money and drop it. When I give money, I want to know what's happening to it. I get involved. I don't know if it's important to anybody else, but the joy you get from seeing what you do is ineffable. Ineffable is my word. Joy beyond description.

I can't tell you how many kids have sent me letters. We have been doing it for years and years. I have a program at Ohio State and at West Virginia.

Here's a picture with a boy on a rock with a note, "I had a wonderful first semester. I had a 3.5 grade point average. Each semester is better than the last ... track is going very well for me. I'm jumping higher than ever—I'm even traveling with the team. Wish you happy holidays and warm weather—it's been freezing up here. Thanks, Ryan Stocking."

He was cute—a red head. He never played in any sports before he came to West Virginia. Now, he's outstanding. What you see is the picture of him climbing a mountain.

My memory is pretty good isn't it? I haven't been to West Virginia in three years. How could I remember all those names?

I worked in this program, because the teachers in West Virginia weren't very good, so neither were our students.

So I offered this scholarship to any student whose parents didn't make more than $40,000 a year, if they had a B average through high school. I knew they wanted an education and we wanted good students and teachers educating our children. I would forgive them the loan for each year they stayed in the state.

Another letter I received was from the person who won the teaching award twice ... Eric Kincaid. Eric taught nanotechnology to seniors in high school at Morgantown High School. He was amazing. No one had ever heard of teaching nanotechnology at that level. Nanotechnology, that's when you can put the whole Bible on the head of a pinhead. It's technological. This happened, because they were teaching it in Israel. He sent for the software, got it, and taught it to his students.

Their letters mean the most to me, because none of the other students keep up with me and I don't know what happened to them. But with these students, I know when they get married, have babies, and get a house. They appreciate it so much more than other students. I appreciate that they keep in touch. It's beautiful.

I try to influence everyone to give.

To convince people how to give, I give speeches. I didn't even know I had this ability until about ten to twelve years ago.

We have three generations of giving now in my family. I skipped my children. I will hand mine down to them. Their children have their own foundation and I want to teach them how to give. I want them to be able to check out who they give funds to and make sure the recipients are doing what they say they're doing. You have to be careful who you give to.

One of our rules is when a company spends more than 20 percent on administration, we don't give them money. If God grants you this money, why wait until you die to give it or give it your family. My family wants me to give my money away. They encourage me. While I've given them money during their lifetime, I haven't given them a lot of money.

It's your responsibility to help people that can't help themselves. I just read about a little school where they are introducing an honors program and every child in that school is on free lunch. The parents don't make enough money to feed their children. Now isn't that terrible. How can a hungry child learn anything when their stomach is empty?

There are many wonderful facilities we have that are truly as honest as can be, like All Faiths Food Bank. What they do for people that are hungry is vital and important.

As I've gotten older, I tell everyone, "Don't wait till you die, give while you live, so you see what good your money is doing."

People come up to me on the street and say, "You taught me how to give." It's the most wonderful feeling in the world.

When I give a speech, it's not a canned speech. Oh my God, It is as real as it can be. I tell people, "Just don't sign a check and say I gave to this cause." Go and find out what good your money is doing and have the thrill of it. I mean, if you give money to all Faiths Food Bank, go to the food bank and see how you have helped.

The joy of giving. The joy I get from giving.

Joy of Giving/Joy of Living

One of the most important things during my lifetime was giving education to children who could not afford it, who are capable of doing beautiful work. From zero to 100 people should always be educated and there should be facilities for them to be educated. You have to continue to learn. You stop using your brain and it deteriorates. You have to use your brain.

I give scholarships at Johnson and Whales Culinary Art School, Ohio State University, one to the school of business, one to the school of education; and one for critical education for women who haven't finished their college. When they're older, I have scholarships for their education, if they can't afford it.

Education and the advancement of Judaism are my two main thrusts in life.

I hope that my children find the joy of giving. I hope they have the means to give. Because with the economy of the world, I'm not sure anybody will be able to give eventually. With the percentage of billionaires, some of them like Bill Gates are giving all his money away, as is Warren Buffet. There are people like that. But there are few amongst all of us.

I feel there is an obligation of those who have wealth to give because people of wealth have such an excess of money. Somebody with something like eight billion dollars. He should keep one billion for himself and give seven billion away to help people who are in positions that they can't help, like people who suffer from poor mental and physical health, like if they have their legs bombed off and they can't get jobs. They should be helping those people. If someone is born with mental illness, people who are bipolar or schizophrenic, those people should be helped. They should have group housing where they live together and learn to manage their bipolar affliction. There are things that they can do in so many areas that can help the world. Babies in Africa are starving. But Africa's another thing. If you save babies from starvation, what are we saving them for? More starvation?

I'm content with the amount of lives I've affected by giving. I think what I've done is—I will use my word—ineffable. I have had joy beyond description from my giving. I just wish I could come back and give twice as much.

When I speak, I try to speak from the heart. That's the only kind that really ever goes over. If you read a speech or teleprompter, it doesn't have the impact of when you speak from here (Points to heart)

You can write an outline, but not the speech. Public speaking is very easy for me. In fact—I like the challenge. I'm not afraid of it like some people are, who consider public speaking, along with death, to be their two biggest fears. I love to get up in front of a group and speak, because I have great messages for people who have the money to give. When I speak, I don't only talk about money—I talk about time, money, and volunteering. Volunteering is very important to agencies that operate on low budgets.

People tell me I'm a good speaker, because I can hold their attention without even trying and when I talk, it's just so natural and it comes from my heart.

When I speak, I just have an outline. My audience is never indifferent. Never indifferent. Why is that? Maybe because

Joy of Giving/Joy of Living

they're amazed that an old woman like me could give them a message like this. I don't know.

My advice for those out there speaking in public is to love the subject that they are trying to give to the public. You have to love the subject. If it is something boring it will come across as boring. If it's something that you're passionate about, show your passion in your speech.

You have to believe it—to sell it. When I spoke in Palm Beach was the first time I knew I had the power of public speaking. I was scared that time. But I thought to myself, "I will tell them just how I feel about giving, and I'll speak from the heart about that." I didn't have a note in front of me. They were eating out of my hand and waiting on my next word.

I still look forward to any opportunities to speak. I love it. When I speak, I have certain things that people like. First of all, I tell everybody to get up and hug each other. Give them a love hug. Then I tell them to raise their hands to the ceiling as high as they can go. Then I wait five seconds and I ask them, "Can you feel he power in this room, how we can change the world?"

And they all go, "WOOOOHHHH!"

Chapter 27

Charleston, West Virginia

"Country roads, take me home
To the place I belong
West Virginia, mountain momma
Take me home, country roads"

— John Denver

Charleston and West Virginia has always meant so much to me and my family. And because of that, we always wanted to give something back to the community.

Many years ago, when my husband was living, one of the first things we did was dedicate a huge gym at the new YMCA they were building. They had one downtown and they decided to put the new one up on a hill.

While the community had tennis courts, as the State Finals approached that were scheduled to be held there, I went to the courts and saw the deplorable condition that they were in and thought, "People from all over the state are coming down here and they will be looking at this terribly run down complex." I offered them money to make some improvements that included resurfacing all courts, adding a refreshment and little snack stand, and building some stands where both the people and those who are judging the tennis can watch. It's called the Schoenbaum Complex for the City of Charleston Tennis Courts.

We also provided funds for the gazebo at Davis Park situated between Washington and Virginia near Summers Street, on the main drag. They performed little concerts there in the summer time. The gazebo we added as part of a beautification of the park is sadly gone now.

We helped with the sculpture at the Civic Center of Charleston. They needed a very tall sculpture so when we went to a show in Miami Beach, we found a 28-foot high sculpture that was perfect. Strangely enough, it was done by a sculptor from Sarasota.

We also endowed the first violin's chair of the West Virginia Symphony Orchestra.

When they built a new structure at the University of Charleston, we funded a new library at this beautiful building facing the Kanawha River. Across from the river, you can see the capitol of Charleston and its gilded dome from the two-and-a-half story library that we funded and we're very proud of that.

We've endowed scholarships at West Virginia University that have been very dear to me personally. The children from West Virginia seem to appreciate the scholarships that we give all over the world more than any other students. As mentioned, they've written wonderful letters of thank you and the continuity of their letters through their lifetime has been a joy to me. I have scrapbooks of all the wonderful letters I've received from the people who we gave scholarships to.

When people ask me about giving joy I have received from giving to education, the letters of thanks that I always bring out to show people are the ones from West Virginia. I give scholarships there to children whose parents do not make more than $40,000 combined. The children are unable to afford school. They have big families and are mostly coal miners. They live in the backwoods and they have nothing to do, but I guess, have children. (Smiles) And so most of them can't go to school.

I have no idea how many scholarships we have provided, but we started it in 1989. It has already been 28 years. The original endowment is still there. I still get beautiful letters from these students.

How does it feel? How would it make you feel, if you had a dozen notebooks like that with page after page of thank you letters of people who could have never gone to college? I feel like I made a difference!

Our good teachers were not staying, because they weren't being paid well. We had a poor grade on our education system in West Virginia because of that lower pay. Now it has accelerated to the point, where we have a good record.

I remember having a discussion in the car with Alex when we drove around town and he said, "You know what? It's a shame that we don't have soccer in Charleston, West Virginia. The United States is so slow in accepting soccer and it's the biggest sport in the world. Every country has soccer teams, but not in the United States. Now I played football and big boys could play football. Tall boys could play basketball. But the average kid could play ping pong."

I remember him saying it isn't fair. "I would love to someday put a soccer field here in Charleston." Well when Alex passed away and I wanted to do something in his memory, I thought, "I'm going to start soccer in Charleston, West Virginia." So I decided to build a stadium with a soccer arena that had 2,000 seats with an amphitheater. On Friday and Saturday nights, families could lay their blankets on the soccer field and hear free band concerts.

The field was made of Astro turf and it was quite an expensive soccer arena to build. There is a place where children could change clothes and people can buy refreshments or bring their own. Children play in the back because with daylight savings time, it's still light when the concert starts. There are Frisbees flying and everything. It's a wonderful family night. In the summertime, the soccer field is used by children from four and five years old all the way through college. It's highly utilized by the colleges, high schools, and families.

Alex was forward thinking in regards to soccer and thought it was a crime that they didn't have it.

In the time, the city built a new entry, which is called Coonskin Park. When you come over the bridge and the Elk River, the first thing that you see is the beautiful soccer stadium and amphitheater.

There's a group that got together many years ago—the Charleston Light Opera Guild that we helped support. In summer, they couldn't have any performances because they didn't have any money. So every summer, I feature two performances, two different productions of the Charleston Light Opera Guild and they've put on shows like *Carousel*, *Chicago*, and *Guys and Dolls*. We've done every famous light opera there is. All very professional.

In fact, we had people so good that they've gone to Hollywood and one is Jennifer Garner. (Brings in picture of Jennifer)

My son-in-law is in love with her. My daughter Joann wanted to surprise him, so she got one of her best friends, who knows Jennifer, to get a picture signed, "To Rick, With Love" for her husband. She hid it in her dresser drawers, until his birthday, but one day he was looking for some socks. He checked her sock drawer for a pair and saw the picture. Well, he loved that picture! I thought it was great of her to do that.

We have brought a lot of culture to Charleston, West Virginia. Charleston is a special to us.

The Kanawha Valley has a river that stretches 15 miles from Charleston and it's the only river that runs the wrong way. You can see coal barges on the river. They are very pretty. When they wash that coal, it gleams in black and is shiny as it sits on those paddle boats.

My husband and I were involved in the Glasser Schoenbaum Center in Sarasota. We saw the need for it and it now serves the needs of over 100,000 people a year. So we decided, we're from Charleston, West Virginia, Why can't we have one in Charleston, West Virginia? So we bought a big building and converted it to a non-profit center with 14 agencies to help people who can't afford services. It services people from age zero to 100.

It has a very good and affordable day school for children. All kinds of services are also provided—much like Glasser

Schoenbaum in Sarasota—housing, homelessness, and hunger. It addresses many things and has agencies that can help people with financial problems. It services a lot of people. It's in a district easy to get to, so they don't have to take a couple of buses to get there. They can get all their needs met in one place. I call it a *mall of human services*. This was my husband's idea to duplicate it here, but unfortunately he didn't live to see it, but I know that he knows it's here.

When the University of Charleston, a lovely private university, constructed a new building, we helped by providing for a new beautiful ballroom, where I've had many of my birthday parties. It sits on the Kanawha River. Across the way, you can see the capital with its gold dome. When they needed a kitchen to serve from, we furnished it for them.

The ballroom is gorgeous. A lot of marble adorns the room, as well as a lot of fine art. We have an abundance of artists in West Virginia—it's a place where artists go to draw and create art, because it's a gorgeous state. The natural environment with our rhododendron in bloom is exquisite.

West Virginia is very bad right now. The coal workers are not working. More people work in coal mining than in any other state. Because of that our coal is not the best coal in the world. The people are buying coal, as cheap as coal is, in other parts of the world. The coal miners are not working, because the owners of the coal mines don't want to bring them up to standard. The owners are from other countries, so they don't care about our coal miners, so now we are having a terrible economic crisis.

I really feel for them, but what can they do? They have lots of kids, but they have no recreation where they live, so *they procreate instead of recreate.*

We had wonderful industries and were the chemical center of the United States during the Second World War. Union Carbon and Carbide had 8,500 employees in the city of South Charleston, which is a suburb of Charleston. When they found out that our river was contaminated by the chemicals created at that time, they had to move their plant, because they couldn't get the river clear. In fact, if you lit a match on the river, it would create a fire on it. It was really terrible. So West Virginia right now is in a very poor economic state.

I still have a big part of my heart here in West Virginia. It always will be. I was there from when I was 23 years old, until I left there when I was 95. I raised my family there and they were glad that they were raised there. They loved it. Our kids could play out in the yard and nobody would touch them. Everything was so safe in Charleston. The kids could go out and ride their bikes all over where we lived in the suburbs.

It just so happens when I raised my children not many women worked. There weren't jobs for women until after World War II, when women went out and worked in factories. After that, many women started working and they worked even if they didn't have to. The husband and wife both worked, so that affected the family. But before that it was heaven. They call it, "Almost Heaven" West Virginia. (Betty starts singing) "Almost Heaven, West Virginia."

I have not been back for a few years. It started getting too difficult, because when you go to West Virginia, you always have to change planes in Charlottesville or Atlanta, which are two horrible hubs to get through if you have a quick change. So often we missed our connection. And the next flight was five hours later.

When I arrived in Charleston, West Virginia, there were 85,000 people in the 1940s. It was the chemical center during the War. Today there about 55,000 people.

We loved Charleston and we loved West Virginia. We sure loved it. It was good to us. We raised our family there and we had our first restaurant there that turned into a national chain.

How could we not give something back?

CHAPTER 28

A Lifetime of Blessings

*"Our prayers should be for blessings in general,
for God knows best what is good for us."*

— Socrates

I don't get in bad moods that much.

But now that I'm older and facing problems that I can't do anything about, I have to face them and just keep going. How do I do that? You just do it. You will yourself. You put thoughts out of your mind and you just keep going forward, so that the rest of your life will be good.

I dwell on the positive and how good my life has been and how beautiful it is now, and I just keep going. And I pray that God gives me more time, so that I can enjoy my family.

I say my prayers at night and have so many names that I have to get through that I fall asleep in the middle of them. When I get up later that night, I finish them. I know where I left off, so I finish the rest of the prayer.

I believe in God so strongly, because I think that the human body is one of the most magnificent things ever created. God fashioned us so we could do all the things that we do. He put brains in us, so that we can think and gave us arms and legs to walk. He's given us this beautiful world that provides us with everything we need that we are destroying. It just strikes me that there is a super being that created it all. How a little spark of energy could have created it all is beyond me, because to be able to create a child who is able to run, walk, talk, and think. Wow! There has to be some supreme being and I call this deity, God.

As I've gotten older, I don't think about questions like, "Does God exist?" We all take some things for granted. Many of us take where we came from for granted. Still you don't think about questions like that all the time, but when you do think about them, it makes you wonder.

During my lifetime, my heart has beat over a billion heartbeats. Who could create a mechanism that can beat 65 times a minute and almost 100,000 beats a day. Who could create someone who lives 365 days a year for 99 years? Wow! It's billions of beats. You just have to believe in a supreme being that has given us this beautiful earth.

What about gravity. Do you know we are one of the few planets that has gravity? If we didn't have gravity, everything that we have would be up in the air floating around. Think about that. You have to realize there is a supreme being. A designer. And now I'm beginning to wonder if our designer isn't angry with us. The reason I think this is the way things are today. We've had terrible tornadoes, tsunamis, hurricanes, volcanoes, and now terrible diseases are spreading around the world killing millions of people. Is God sending these plagues until we get back to loving instead of hating each other. I don't think he made the world for people to hate each other.

Every human being has a bad habit or two—my worst habit is procrastination. That's largely because I can't get to some things, because I'm so busy. If you saw my mail every day. It's procrastination. I am procrastinating today while I'm talking to you. I have a dozen phone calls to make and six thank you notes to write.

I am busy and as I get older and slower, I procrastinate more. I guess I have to just ask God for more hours in the day. (Laughs)

My best habit is an appreciation of what I have and my mood is up most of the time. But now that I'm older and can't do everything that I want to do, I'm a little down. Now I appreciate when people can't come to meetings and everything, because they're not well. I'm facing this adjustment right now. I'm just appreciative of my life. I feel so blessed to have all these wonderful children, grandchildren, and great-grandchildren and to be able to enjoy them and be a part of their lives. I've been blessed to have the years to do it. And I'm still blessed. Truly blessed.

People will be surprised, but my definition of a perfect day is when I don't have anything to do, because usually I am so busy. It would be a gift. So the perfect day is not having anything to do. I know that's a contradiction. I know it is. But I have it so seldom that it's a gift.

I've got a lot of great-grandchildren—nine and number 10 is on his way. Four children. Eight grandchildren. I don't favor any one over the other and I love them all the same.

They're all the same. They're my children's children. They're my children. They're my great-grandchildren. I love them all the same. I have the joy of seeing them grow up.

The centerpiece in my life is my family. Number One. My giving is secondary. Family means everything to me. With me, I think how blessed I have been to have lived to see all this happen. This is unbelievable for me that God gave me all these years. Look at this picture.

Just think if I didn't marry Alex Schoenbaum none of these people would be here. Think of what the world would be missing!

I just feel that way about every person in here. (Points to picture) My children happen to marry nice people. My son-in-law and my two daughters-in-law—sometimes I say I love them more than my children, because they put up with my children. (Laughs)

When I hold their hands and we're in a circle together I can feel love going all the way around the circle through our fingers. It's just unbelievable.

As I look at this photo and consider how much of this is fate, destiny, or luck? I think I would have married somebody else. (Laughs) I would still have had offspring. But looking at these people and seeing what they have done in their lives, I am so proud that I started it all.

We started the tree. This boy here, Brian (points to picture), was honored by Forbes as one of the outstanding young men in the country. He's gorgeous. And look at this one here. My grandchildren are gorgeous. Here they are, one two, three, and four. Look at their faces. Four tall men—all gorgeous.

That's Jamie in the center and she married Adam.

I never take any of this for granted. No, I never do. I just feel like I was blessed. My lesson to the kids is not to take things for granted. Children live by example. That is the most important thing that I learned about life. Children learn by example. So they need to have good parents who love them and are concerned about them, and don't spoil them with material things.

If Alex saw this picture, I have to tell you he would be wishing that his deceased brother, Raymond, had lived to have a family like he had. He wouldn't think of himself, but he worried about that boy who got killed at age 30. Alex never got over his brother's death. They were eleven months apart in age. Alex had a broken heart about his brother for his whole life. He never felt like he deserved all this. All the blessings and things in life. He had a sadness in him from the day his brother died.

I consider myself a blessed girl from Ohio. I'm always an Ohioan. I was born and bred in Ohio. My family lived in Ohio—my grandparents migrated there in the 1880s. And I had a big family there. My father came from a family of seven children. I had a lot of relatives there in Ohio and I spent my college years there. I met Alex there and we lived in Columbus. West Virginia was a wonderful time in my life and I love that state. It is beautiful and just a gorgeous state.

I have been blessed to have really three places where I lived and could call home. From birth to 22 years old, I spent my life in Ohio. From 23, I moved to West Virginia and lived there for 74 years. I moved to Sarasota in 1975. While spending a lot more time in Florida, we still spent part of the year in West Virginia, until a couple years ago.

There are beautiful things about each place—Florida, West Virginia, and Ohio.

The best of Ohio would be my relationship with my family, because we had a big family in Ohio. Lots of cousins, aunts, and uncles, lots of wonderful time together, and a wonderful childhood, a wonderful life.

In West Virginia, you have your children, your friends who have children the same age as your children, and you made lots of friends. And when you are in a smaller community, friends are really important, because we didn't have as much family there, although we had Alex's family, because Alex had lived there since he was ten.

The best of Florida is living in Sarasota, Florida. It offers you the best of everything you want. If you want to be active, they have something for you do. For entertainment, everything is top-notch. The symphony is top, as is our ballet, dramatics, art, Mote Marine, and our Ringling complex. Everything, everything we do, even athletes, are top-notch now, with our recent international rowing event at Benderson Park, which put us on the map internationally. When you get Olympic Trials—that's big time.

Another important thing about Sarasota is the people. They have big hearts. In fact, Sarasota County is the most giving county in the United States per capita. We give more, per capita to non-profits, than any other place in the United States.

The Joy of Giving is the Joy of Living

I've been blessed with some good habits. I'll tell you one of my good habits—I think of what I can do to help people. When I see the problems that people are having, I just want to help them and thank God I have funds that I can dip into, to a certain point, to start something and see that it gets finished. This to me is the best habit that I have.

Like this morning, I got up and said I have to call my foundation in West Virginia and give them some additional funds, because our soccer field's Astro turf started breaking down because of heavy rains and years of wear and tear.

It's important that you have a purpose every day. I have a lot of purposes, because I am on a lot of boards and I attend meetings. I get involved. And I've been blessed to be able to get involved in life. When you give money to something, you should know about it. You should get on the board of these groups, so that you can know what they're doing with your money and how it's helping people.

Chapter 29

World Views & the Meaning of Life

"The sole meaning of life is to serve humanity."

— Leo Tolstoy

The meaning of life.

I feel God places you on earth and what you do with your life is up to you.

I have found during my lifetime, that to be kind and help underprivileged people is one the most important things in our lives. If we have money to give, we should be giving it to that cause. My main contributions go to help the underprivileged. I do this because someday the USA will consist of just the rich and the poor, if we don't look out for these underprivileged people and give them the tools to become middle class.

The biggest problem with this country is we don't have a big enough middle class. The middle class used to be a larger percentage of our people. Those are the people that buy the refrigerators, cars, and houses and keep our economy going. There are so few rich people. I mean how many refrigerators do they need? Not many. And the poor people can't afford them. So we have to make more of a middle class. That's why the United States became successful after the Second World War. They offered a college education in the form of the GI Bill to every person who was in the service. That's what built our large middle class. Those people are now baby boomers and are retiring, causing this big building boom.

Someone I have always looked up to—Harry S. Truman. If any of our presidents were "for the people, of the people and by the people," it was Truman. I liked him. I really did. I'm an independent and he was from Independence, Missouri. He was a true man and a great leader.

To me education is everything. It is my belief that some of the Muslim people don't believe in education as much, simply because it was not stressed to them as much. Maybe I'm wrong, but I feel the Muslim fathers don't want their children to be smarter than they are. That is the opposite of what most parents wish for their children—they want their children to be smarter and more successful. I want them to use everything that God gave them, especially their brains, to make this a better world and not a world where people hate each other. I think that people need to turn more toward loving each other and accepting people as they are. We're not all perfect.

I've often thought, "What happens to us after we leave the planet?"

I believe there is an energy that's left. I don't know what happens. Whether you call it your spirit—I do believe that there is life after death. I guess I'm crazy, but so many people do believe that when you die you go to heaven and you meet your family again. Do you know how many spirits are in heaven? Billions and trillions of people have died in this world and their spirits went up there? How are you going to find your family? Huh?

What happens? I'm not sure what happens.

I think the bad dies in you and the good lives on. I think you're remembered by your deeds and by what you have done for others on earth. Not for yourself, but for others. Definitely.

One of the big problems today is greed. Right across the board. Even the heads of Lehman Brothers. Big people. Big people. Cheated.

What does fame mean to me? I find out famous people are just regular people. Folks back then had much more integrity and morals. Aside from Gerry Ford and Max Fisher, a man who impressed me was Jay Rockefeller IV, the United States Senator from West Virginia. We knew him well. He had a fine education in foreign affairs especially China and Japan.

Nature is still important to me today. I notice the trees when they get green and shiny and when there is not enough rain for them. I watch them when they get brown. I'm always aware of nature.

When I speak to the great-grandchildren, I tell them, "That's what God created for us." People don't realize that the reason this earth is here is because the hot core in the center of our earth causes gravity. If all of a sudden that cools off—we float off into space. Everything. Everything here in this place. Did you ever think of it that way?

I'm still very much that little girl on that cottage from my youth. I loved it. But in reality, I'm not the same person. I've grown so much. Grown—but my roots are still there and they will never leave that little cottage.

I hope that my grandkids have an appreciation of nature.

Definitely. Just look outside at all there is to see.

As I look outside at my view and at Sarasota's future.

It's becoming overcrowded and leading to the demise of the downtown area. If I had a magic wand, I'd take all these cranes away. (Laughs) That little key, Golden Gate Point, used to be a charming key of little houses.

Looking at the tiny park below us is where Embracing Our Differences has their exhibit. I have a poster that I sponsored there. I haven't seen it yet this year but I put a poster there every year since its inception.

It's important to do, because I remember my husband saying, "We are all descended from Abraham, Isaac, and Jacob and we are all brothers all over the world." Then he added, "And when we have a war, we're killing our own brothers."

That little park exhibit does so much good and it tries to prove that we are brothers and sisters, no matter our race, creed, or color. Some of those are really marvelous. We started that in Sarasota and now it's around the world. It is a way to open up people's eyes, especially children's eyes, through education.

It's wonderful. You should see the buses all month that roll up here. They spend a half-day there and get an explanation and an education. Thousands of kids attend. It's a great thing for race relations.

I'm an optimist. Is my cup half-full? My cup is running over all the time. All the time. I'm an optimist, but I'm pessimistic when I need to be. Yet I am hopeful that when people can sit down and tell their differences, then they can solve them. But when they are adamant and won't change, then we won't be able to change a thing.

I believe in diplomacy, but what we did in Iran, giving them ten more years to make the bomb was the stupidest thing that this world ever did. The United States never should have greenlighted that. And now we can't stop them.

What does love mean to me? You can't really describe love. It's an emotion. It goes deeper than description. I don't give to have people love me. I give, because I love to give. In fact, I don't care what you think of me—if I like you, I like you.

Ray Kroc was famous for saying, "Keep it simple stupid." We knew Ray Kroc and his wife well and they were both very generous. Ray Kroc believed in a clean parking lot, too, and was very impressed with how the original McDonald brothers kept it so clean. That's why my husband was so good—he taught our boys to scrape the gum off the parking lot.

Keeping it simple. I never wanted a claim to fame. I didn't want to be famous or well known or anything. It just happens with the things that you do that go along with your claims. I don't claim anything.

My joy is in the giving. I'm interested in people. I get bored when I have to stay home all day when I'm not well. If I'm not busy I feel like I'm not helping people.

Regarding my grandchildren and accomplishing a successful life, I hope that they help people. Don't live just for yourself. Help other people that can't help themselves. Give them a helping hand, whether it is by money, physical things you do for them, whatever. Give of yourself to make other people's lives better.

The homeless problem for instance is one problem that can be solved. It just takes money. I would be the first to recognize that not all these people want help. If that's what they choose, then leave them alone. You're not going to force them to do it. A bed and food is not the answer—you have to go further. They have to have some consultation that can show them how to get over it. How you get a job.

I don't agree with what Freud said, "If you can love and work, you can have a normal life." I think that a lot of people who work, don't know how to love.

My mantra I live by is,

The joy of giving is the joy of living.

That can be in the form of time or financial help, or just saying nice things to people to give them a lift for the day. It's nice to do. When I see a waitress who's waiting on me, I'm thinking she probably has a couple of kids at home, no husband, and everything, and she works so hard. Say something nice. If she has pretty eyes—tell her. If her service is good, you tell her. You don't make a lie up, but you tell her to make her feel good. The lift that it gives the girl. Here she is, she's dead-tired and it makes her feel good. It only takes a second.

Today I'm going to an event with Joy Weston. Quite a gal. She is speaker, who's talking about, "How to get the most out of life." Fantastic. For me, I get the most out of life by *helping people.*

I help people because they need help. I don't belong to fancy organizations. I belong to the Woman's Resource Center, Glasser-Schoenbaum, and Salvation Army board—those aren't glamourous. They're for the underprivileged. They speak to me the most, as do my early education and scholarships. That's my thing. You heard about my books. Well, I have a second closet with thank you letters. I've read them all. (Smiles) But now I can't keep up.

I want to be remembered as a giving person. Whether a compliment, financial aid, sitting down and praying with them, or giving them a hug—it's just helping people. Wouldn't it be nice if everyone was like that? What a beautiful world.

It's important to be curious if you want to learn. Yet we can overdo it—all the machines, smart phones, and stuff. I don't have one. I don't know how to text and I don't want to know. But I know how to neck, from the neck up. (Laughs) Neck I did.

I know what texting is. All I see is everybody going with their fingers this way and that way. I see my two- and three-year-old grandchildren texting and I feel horrible about that. They learn to do these things so good that they do it all day. They sit there all day. A two-year-old watching cartoons and getting anything that she wants on her machine. She's learned how to do it and knows if she presses this button and that button, she gets what she wants, but she loses something—reading about it.

I see families sit down in restaurants and the kids get their devices out and the parents don't say a word. They don't say, "We are going to sit down and have a conversation. We're not going to have those things out." Truth is, the parents want the kids quiet and doing what they want. It's easier for the kids to text than it is to sit at the table, talk, argue, and fight. There is no interaction with the family. And that's terrible. Even when they are eating dinner. If I had children today, I would tell them to park those in the hallway when you walk into this house.

There are people walking down the street texting. You see

"scads" of people. People go out to lunch and they are sitting by themselves and they are texting the whole time. WOW! I mean Wow.

In some positive ways—it's affected innovation. Universities are putting up buildings called innovation buildings. You go to school and learn how to use your brain in new ways. You can't look it up texting. I have never used Google, but my secretary, Ray, pulled up what's on Google about me. I don't email. Ray does it all. I have seen so many phases of technology throughout my life. From the typewriter to the iPhone.

I'm one of the luckiest people in history to live in the 20th century, where we had no airplanes, autos just happened, industrial revolution was beginning, and the information highway with the computers and everything. This has been the most outstanding century for things to happen in the history of the world. Think about it.

That's the plus side. The things we accomplished. We got to the moon. We've done so many things. We developed our brains to be able to do it. Now machines are being developed to do it. We don't even have to use our brains.

There are positives and negatives—a lot of negatives. Our society has completely changed. The biggest thing that has changed is when our big firms who make billions of dollars of business and they still cheat. Integrity is gone. They can cheat and hide it and they do cheat and hide it. Look at Lehman Brothers and so many others.

There are no answers. People are used to that now. They can't live without it. Kids are texting away their lives—they don't seem to know how to live without it. I was born in the last century. I have seen more changes in the last 100 years than at any other time in history.

I worry about things that will affect my great-grandchildren. I worry about the climate and what we found out about the climate with so many countries not doing anything about it. If we don't do something, this world will not be able to survive.

Do I believe that I'm leaving the world a better place?

Certainly. But we better all start doing it or there's not going to be a world. If we let people like ISIS put such fear in us, that we are afraid to even open our mouths or we will get killed.

The message I delivered today was to empower women. It's very hard for a woman to get there. When you hear these women who are heads of these big corporations, say, "Oh it will never work." Some of them have been real leaders and have taken their companies far along the way. Women should get equal pay as do the men for the same job, period.

I don't read as much as I used to, because I have macular degeneration. I strain my eyes for the news that I want to read. My eyes are getting bad right now. When I was young, I was an avid reader. I would read five books a week. I lived near the library. My sister was a big tease and to forget her, I would read. I would sit away from her and just read. That's why I have a good vocabulary. When I would read, I would have a dictionary right next to me and anytime I didn't know a word, I'd look it up. That's how I found ineffable. I'm also very good at math. Sometimes I can do math faster than a computer.

As I enter the last chapters of my life, what I would love to change about the world is this: *I want people to love each other as much as they hate and to forget about hatred.* You know, I have this love hug and I'm trying to spread it around the world. A heart-to-heart hug. It's the best feeling in the world, because you have exchanged a hug with them. So I give you a gift and you give me a gift when we hug. That's what I want, people to give each other goodness instead of hatred.

I have helped thousands of people. It's given me ineffable joy. Joy beyond description. I had the heart to give somebody money and how it helped their lives. It's a marvelous feeling. Marvelous.

What do I think happens to us after we leave here? I think there is an energy that a person has and the more energy you have, the more beautiful it is and your soul and spirit prevails. I don't know where this place could be. I believe it's energy and they use that energy for something else.

The good positive energy goes to one place and the negative energy goes to another place, not all to one place. Look we don't know how we were created. We each are a miracle. Each one of us. You're a miracle and I'm a miracle. When you see what this body can do from a little seed. Huh? Sperm and an egg. We were created. Look at us. We walk. We talk. We shut our eyes. We open our mouths. We go to sleep. We bathe ourselves. We are able to have babies. We are able to do everything.

Do I believe in an intelligent designer? I believe in a supreme being. Is someone saying, "The world needs a Betty and Alex Schoenbaum. They're going to meet and she's going to say, 'Listen, Alex, you better get that job over there selling cars.' Well I don't think it goes like that. That's a fantasy. But I know it happened.

There is a supreme being who created us. It had to be. We couldn't just come from a fusion of this and that. Look at my heart. Who invented my heart? My heart has beaten over two billion heartbeats. My heart beats every hour. OK, my heart beats 99,000 heart beats every 24 hours. Do you know what your heart beats every minute? Well mine beats, I have a slow heart, 3900 times, almost 4,000. That's about 96,000 heart beats a day. Now 365 times 96,000 times 98 for my years, and I'm roughly 2,600,000,000 heartbeats. Now who could invent something like that? Only a supreme being.

I believe in what Einstein said, "God doesn't play dice with the universe." I do. It can happen. When they were making us, they made mistakes and they had to do them over. We eat food. We defecate it. It doesn't stay in us. It goes out of us and as it does, it doesn't contaminate us. That's unbelievable. We're unbelievable.

Does that prove that a Supreme Being exists? No, I haven't proved a thing.

But I have faith that something exists and I call it God. I pray to God each and every day.

Chapter 30

My Family Tree & Me

"A happy family is but an earlier heaven."

— George Bernard Shaw

I'm so proud of my family.

They're beautiful people both inside and out. And they're good people.

My mother and daddy were the best, the absolute best. My daddy was a businessman. He had four older brothers—he was the baby and they treated him like the baby all his life.

Let's talk about my family a bit. Let's start with my brothers and sisters. We always had a beautiful family feeling. There were four children born in seven years. And my parents never sent us to camp, because they wanted us to be together and play with each other and be at home, so that they could enjoy us. My daddy loved fishing, boating, and gardening. My mother loved to cook and take care of her children. We loved to go out to the cottage in the summertime. They let us play like kids who were farm kids. We milked cows, rode horses, sat on reapers, and we mowed the hay down. We swam and fished every day.

My oldest brother was Joe Frank, who died at 90. My sister, Geri, died at 92. I have a brother, Marvin, who is 94 and I'm 99.

Joe had a great sense of humor, just a great sense of humor. When you were with Joe, you laughed all the time. He married a lovely woman. They couldn't have children, so they adopted two children, one of whom became a nurse and the other became a doctor. Joe made you feel good. Joe was happy.

My oldest sibling was Geri, 21 months older than me. Her real name was Phyllis Geraldine, but she didn't like it. So then she went to Geraldine and then Geri when she went into the theater. Fortunately, I got taller than her. But up to that time I wore her hand-me-downs.

Was it a friendly competition between sisters? Well, no, not really. I'd rather not talk about that. I loved her, but she would always say, "You won't get married". She continued by saying, "You look like an old woman," because when it looked like it was going to rain, I carried an umbrella to school. She made the National Honor Society as a junior and I didn't make it until I was a senior.

I started to build my self-esteem when I got to college and started winning cups for my dancing. The piano in the sorority house had one cup after another that I'd won sitting on top of it from competitions.

On July 23, 2017 I was honored by Alpha Epsilon Phi Society RHO chapter as National Alumni of the year in Norfolk, Virginia, at their convention three months short of my 100th birthday.

The boys liked me a lot. My first quarter of school, I was dated all the way to Christmas in two weeks. (Laughs) My dance card was filled up for dates on the weekends. I knew I had something. I knew the boys liked me, but I didn't put out either. No sir. As I have said, "We necked. And necking is from the neck up." That's the truth.

My sister, Geri, didn't want to go to college. She wanted to be a ballerina. We studied dancing every summer in New York from the age of 14 to 18. My mother would take us and we would stay at a French Hotel, The St. George Hotel in Brooklyn. At that time it was pretty new. I'm talking about the early 1930s. We went to dancing school on 57th street, at the Chalif School which was right across from Carnegie Hall. It was renowned for ballet. They were wonderful summers and we were there for six weeks.

In New York, well we had automats and a lot of delis. We had the big white way, which was Broadway. I was just 14 years old so I'm not going to view it like other people. I was really a child at that time. It wasn't like today. We studied dancing every day and we had no air conditioning. But I really loved dancing. And my sister adored it and made it her career. Geri wanted to be a ballet dancer, a ballerina dancer, and that was her goal in life. She got quite high up there and then the show went on the road. When it got down to New Orleans, they were having some kind of problem with mosquitoes, and my parents decided that a nice Jewish girl didn't go around from city to city and travel like that and sleep in different beds every week. She ended up getting malaria, so my parents would not allow her to go back after studying dancing for 17 years, from the time she was five until she was 22. They made her come home, which kind of broke her spirit. She used to tease me and tell me that I would never find a husband, but I was married five years before she did.

We were getting closer when she moved out to California. She lived there after she had her first child, while I stayed in West Virginia. Her children are about the same age as my children. Sadly we didn't see each other as much as we would have. You didn't travel across country like you do today, because the planes would stop two or three times before you got to the West Coast. It was around 1941.

Unfortunately she strangled on a pill at the hospital and when they gave her the Heimlich maneuver she became paralyzed in her hands and her legs. They cut her spinal cord and while she got use of her hands back in time, she never got the use of her legs back and was confined to a wheelchair for the last ten years of her life. For a dancer, that was a terrible thing. She lived a good long life, but the last ten years were hard for her. Sadly my sister ended up being very angry for the rest of her life, because of what the hospital did to her.

She could never get over the anger. They settled with the hospital, but it only paid for a year of her time in the nursing home where she lived the last ten years of her life. She was bitter. She tried a lot of therapy, but sadly she had no way to make it better, because she couldn't get on her feet.

My brother, Marvin, was gorgeous. Oh, my God, wait till you see his picture. Oh, just gorgeous! He's six feet two and is still living. He lived in Naples, Florida, for about 25 years, but he was from Lexington. At one time, he had 27 men's clothing stores at colleges. As people started wearing no socks, flip flops, and t-shirts to school, he closed his shops, because there was no need. In his day, when we went to school, he had to wear a jacket and tie. His stores were called The University Shops but some were called Marvin's Men's Wear. Mostly the shops were in Ohio, but he also had one in Clemson, one in North Carolina, and one in South Carolina. The only store that still remains is the one at Clemson, which is now owned and operated by one of his managers.

Whenever I see Marvin, what did we talk about? We talked about our beautiful lives at Crystal Lake when we are growing up. We talk about the lake every time we are together. We lived out there during the summer when we didn't go to camp. We would drop our lines down at the clubhouse with our bait in it and the next morning, we would go down and see what we caught. We were on a little bitty hill. We could see the clubhouse and we would run down the hill, when we were both little children.

That cottage didn't have running water or electricity. The cottage was so sparse compared to the luxury I live in today, but we also had that beautiful English Tudor home in Dayton, Ohio.

But back to the cottage, it was beautiful, because the family was together.

It's family. It's something no one can take away from you. A lot of people don't have a family like that. Today the parents go golfing and the kids go to camp. It's different.

It's harder to keep a family together today. I think it's easier to live a life like I lived—when we all sat down to dinner every night and we didn't have anybody texting at the table. After dinner, we stayed at the dinner table and talked about our day. My daddy would talk about his day. It was family. We were very much together. Then Amos and Andy would come on at 7 o'clock and we would all sit down at the breakfast room table again, because it was close. We were close. We would sit close like that and put the radio in the middle of the table. We listened to the radio. There was no television. We spent time together. We shared our lives with each other. Beautiful. Beautiful. Beautiful!

Now I'm going to tell you a cute story about the whole thing. Every Sunday, they would take all four of us to the movies and they would go home. We always wondered when we got older, "When did our parents have sex?" We decided that it was every Sunday afternoon. (Laughs) While we were in the movies. My parents would take us to the movies and tell us to go to the ice cream place after the movies and wait for them.

But maybe I shouldn't put that in this book.

Every week we'd see a movie. Yes one movie. And I do remember the first movie I saw, which was Al Jolson, *The Jazz Singer*. I saw him when I was 10 years old. What a revelation. Instead of reading the script below on the screen, you could hear him. And then when color came in—wow!

They had gorgeous movies that nowadays would cost too much to make. *Broadway Melody*. Spectaculars with dancing. Esther Williams. Those were spectacular movies. I remember back then. Wow! That was a revelation.

I loved Cary Grant. I have a cute story about that. When I was pregnant with Raymond, I was so in love with Cary

Grant, that when I would go to movies, I'd sit with my middle finger and index finger and make a cleft in my chin. For the whole movie I would be sitting there with a cleft in my chin. Well, what has happened since? Raymond was born with a cleft in his chin, and nobody in our family had a cleft in their chin. And now his granddaughter has a cleft in her chin. (Laughs) I thought Cary Grant was just gorgeous.

Everybody told me that I looked like Bette Davis when I was young and some other people said I looked like Joan Crawford. I don't know. But my sister did look like Joan Bennet.

The movies back then were different compared today's films. I'll tell you. We never saw anybody in bed with each other. And when we did see people who were married, they all had twin beds. Mary Tyler Moore and Dick Van Dyke had twin beds and they wore pajamas. Plain pajamas. People were dressed and clad. They show entirely too much today. The nudity and everything. They do that to attract people to go see it. It has nothing to with the theme. The stories back then were wholesome. There were no cuss words, not a foul mouth, no put down of people. It was wonderful, just wonderful.

Most of the moguls were Jewish and adhered to Judea Christian values. Most of them, 99 percent were Jewish. I have a niece who gives speeches about that. Paramount, MGM, Fox, Warner Brothers—they were all Jewish. They tried to put something out there that was different and it was very competitive. We didn't even hear the word damn.

The media has a big influence in shaping morals and mores of today. They are the ones who have destroyed it. They have literally destroyed the morals of society. They used to have those movies on late at night. Now you can see sex on television at 9 o'clock. Kids are rushed into growing up quicker.

When they play an older movie, they are absolutely beautiful movies. Now every other word is a cuss word. I don't go to movies anymore.

Some of my favorite movies?

I love anything with Fred Astaire. I loved *The Red Shoes*. I loved anything with dancing. All those spectaculars with dancing. I remember one with the staircase and the gorgeous girls, each one with beautiful costumes. I wonder what that would cost to stage now. The studios probably couldn't afford it today.

In our family, we have a new baby that's just come into the world. I wish for him what I wish for all my children, and all children of the world. A better world. It's not a good world. Our world is sick. There's not one place that's not infected by what's happening in this world.

Certainly, I do think that the Radical Islam is the biggest threat to the world. Why certainly. Because of the bomb that they have—the radicals. They can destroy New York completely. One hit and it could all be gone.

I worry about all that.

And at night when I say my prayers for all my wonderful family and friends, I also pray for the world.

Chapter 31

Ineffable Joy

"Gratitude is the sign of noble souls."

— Aesop

Ineffable Joy means joy beyond description.

It is Betty's favorite term, word and expression.

And one that aptly describes her incredible, long and blessed life.

Ineffable joy.

Betty Schoenbaum gets it, because Betty lives it. And of course Betty gives it.

Ineffable joy to everyone who comes into her presence.

On this day the woman from Dayton surely had it.

Ineffable Joy.

And it wasn't because they had thrown her a birthday party in honor of her 99th year on earth. No, Betty Schoenbaum was smiling ear to ear, dressed to the nines, in her case her "99s," because many of the people that mattered to her most, her family and friends, were all there with her to celebrate the day together.

Ineffable Joy.

Ineffable Joy

You could see it in her face as she greeted each and every guest. Some she knew since birth, others for decades, and only a few she met on this day. But the reaction was—as it always is with the great lady.

Betty was grateful for her guests.

Her words of appreciation were sincere.

And the joy on her face was ineffable.

There's that word again—ineffable joy.

Evident in her demeanor, as she counted her blessings on this day from the countless guests.

It was billed as a "*Hat's Off to Betty*" party.

Guests were asked to bring merely their presence and wear a favorite hat to the party that they would remove as part of a toast and tasteful gesture in tribute to this woman named Betty, who has worn so many hats over her long and blessed life.

Guests were asked to bring their hats and possibly a brief joke to share with her and her guests on this special day.

And that's exactly what many of them did. They shared a joke or two with the crowd, all in an effort to please the guest of honor.

Judging by her smile and laughter that came straight from her heart, Betty was pleased.

She delighted in her daughter Emily's creative poetry and prose. She laughed as her oldest son, Raymond, channeled all the great Borsch Belt comedians with his wit, jokes and storytelling ability. All that was missing was the drummer. She smiled as her daughter, Joann, worked the room like only she can. She smiled proudly as her grandson delivered a joke and humbly said that he had to work on his delivery next time. She laughed from her toes to the top of her hat as old friends and family alike shared the best jokes all in an effort to bring a smile to her face.

And in the end it was a complete success.

The setting was spectacular. The treats and eats were outstanding. And the company, well, the company is where it was all at—for Betty.

On this day, the day she would celebrate her 99th birthday, all that she wanted as a present was simple—she wanted their presence.

That was the gift that she wanted.

That was the gift that she got.

Their presence.

To sit down for a little while, amongst family and friends and make some new memories and share others just like she once did, so many years ago at a little cottage on a lake.

Back there and then, with family and friends, she gathered to enjoy the day and take it all in.

The funny thing is that from here, high atop the high-rise condo where she calls home, she can still see that little cottage on the lake.

And because of that, now all those many years later, she was doing the same things she did when she was a little girl on the lake.

She was still experiencing her life, her grand, big, wonderful and blessed life with that same timeless smile on her face and with ineffable joy in her heart.

Chapter 32

Happy 100th Birthday to Our Beautiful Betty!

"Ain't she sweet..."

How does one plan a birthday party fit for a Queen? The answer is—constantly, with great care and compassion and with a concerted team effort headed by a master party planner—Betty's very own daughter—Joann Schoenbaum Miller.

But make no mistake about it—this was total team, total family, friend, and in many cases, total country effort, as help came from all directions of the world to help in the planning and execution of a series of parties to celebrate the ineffable joy of one Betty Schoenbaum for her 100th birthday. And why should it not? Her long and glorious life has stretched, like tentacles of a giving octopus in multiple directions—helping anyone and everyone in her reach.

So on this day, September 27, 2017, her actual birthday—Betty greeted a small gathering of family, friends, and the media as she accepted a proclamation from the Mayor of Sarasota declaring this day—September 27th—"Heart-to-Heart Hug Day in Sarasota."

As the great lady entered the room she hummed, the old tune, "Ain't she sweet."

The Joy of Giving is the Joy of Living

A few hours later, for the second gathering of over 100 or so of her friends, Betty entertained from the penthouse of her beautiful apartment. There she waved down to street level 18 floors below to a myriad of the organizations that she has helped and been a part of spreading her gifts of giving. There they gathered to give her a private parade and extend birthday wishes. Even from the street, you could see this grand gal's broad smile. Ineffable joy indeed.

Still, it had become the biggest event of her 100th Birthday Celebrations. Nearly 300 people gathered at Michael's On East, and in the grand ballroom for a party to end all parties.

Once again she entered the room, humming her signature song "Ain't She Sweet" to throngs of family, friends, and fans of the great dame from Dayton. Infectious smiles filled the room as tributes were orchestrated from nearby tables filled with loving organizations, friends and, of course, family. Speeches were abundant and heartfelt. Tributes included a video birthday wish from West Virginia's own—Actress Jennifer Garner and a birthday wish from Alex Trebek of Jeopardy TV fame in the form of a question. Heck—Betty even got a birthday wish and tribute from the Ohio State University—on the scoreboard between the second and third quarters of their football game. The tributes were extensive and overwhelming.

But while leaving Betty in awe, it didn't leave the great lady speechless.

She still was up to giving a great speech that would thank everyone. Especially her large and very demonstrative family, led by each and every one of her grandchildren and great-grandchildren, who wore numbered shirts to remind everyone of the true and lasting legacy of this great lady. Her family. She laughed as Sarah (Number 5) while trying to do her best to finish a rap song with the rest of the family, said, "Jews don't rap."

Grandma laughed. Smiled. And in between tributes, speeches, bits and proclamations gave a 1000 WOW's of approval. Ineffable Joy. Ain't she sweet ...

You could see and feel the love in the room.

It was complete and authentic love and admiration for a great lady. All deserved for a woman with a great family who has been a family to many in her glorious life.

As she sat down at the family table, you just felt that she would burst with joy. In many ways, it reminded one of a giant kid's table with Betty sitting at its head—the biggest kid of them all, still young at heart even now at her round age of 100 years.

Sitting there at a table surrounded by her children, grandchildren, and great grandchildren, it was little bit of the old cottage days brought indoors. This family table, and in essence this kid's table—a glorious table of love that was set by one—Betty Schoenbaum— and, of course, her late husband, Alex, who was looking down on the festivities in spirit and captured in the form of a "Big Boy" cutout that helped decorate the room.

Something Betty has often said as she's looked back fondly at a wedding picture of her big family echoed in my head. As I watched her creating new memories and photos with that same family on this special day, I remembered what Betty had told me on many occasions: "If it wasn't for Alex and me getting together, this would not have been possible. This whole group of people happened because of us."

A few days after all the parties and before the plans for her next one have been started, she shared her thoughts.

"Oh my God, I looked up at that stage at my party, when all my grandchildren and great-grandchildren were crowded up there, because they are all big people, for their age, even the little guy. When I saw them up there, I said how Oh, my God, how many people can look up there and see their family? See their life, their whole life from ages one to 47, and say they're all mine, they're all mine. And I thank you God for blessing me this way."

On this day, this giver of much for human kind was glad to take a little, as she took in the true meaning of her legacy.

This tree of people.

Her family tree.

One that she created with a big boy named Alex.

Together they created a whole family of good, giving people and that is her final and greatest gift to the world in a lifetime of giving.

It is something that will last for years—maybe hundreds of years—this legacy started by this little girl from Dayton named Betty Schoenbaum.

That's why she was smiling and about to burst with joy as she celebrated. It was not so much her 100th birthday, but for her big, beautiful, adoring family that she helped create, and has enjoyed and been grateful for, each and every day of her wonderful life.

Appendix

OFFICES HELD:
President, The Schoenbaum Family Foundation, Inc.

CURRENT BOARD MEMBERSHIPS HELD:
American Jewish Committee,
The Ohio State University Foundation (lifetime)
Glasser/Schoenbaum Human Services Center,
The Salvation Army Advisory Board.
Jewish Federation Sarasota-Manatee,
The Schoenbaum Family Foundation, Inc.

COMMITTEE MEMBERSHIPS:
Jewish Federation Sarasota-Manatee Scholarship Committee

PHILANTHROPIES:
Numerous major philanthropic gifts by Mr. and Mrs. Alex Schoenbaum when Mr. Schoenbaum was alive include:

- Through The Schoenbaum Fund established in 1973 at Greater Kanawha Valley Foundation in Charleston,

- West Virginia, purchased sports and recreation equipment for over 207 public schools in the Charleston area, as well as funded many other diversified causes, with funding continuing annually for diversified projects in Charleston, West Virginia.

- Major contributors of a gymnasium to the YMCA in Charleston, West Virginia.
- Presented the City of Huntington, West Virginia, with a floating stage on the Ohio River.
- Funding for a Gazebo in Davis Park in Charleston, West Virginia.
- Founded and funded The Schoenbaum Scholarship Foundation.
- Built a library in Tel Mond, Israel.
- Major contributors to Glasser/Schoenbaum Human Services Center of Sarasota.
- Major contributors to Temple Beth Sholom in Sarasota for a religious center.
- Funded the Alex and Betty Schoenbaum Administrative and Volunteer Complex at All Faiths Food Bank in Sarasota.
- Funded an administration building which is named Schoenbaum Hall at Kiski Prep School, Saltsburg, Pennsylvania.
- Major contribution to The Salvation Army Territorial Development Fund.
- Fully funded a sculpture in front of the Civic Center in Charleston, West Virginia.
- Fully endowed a First Violinist Chair for the West Virginia Symphony Orchestra.

THE SCHOENBAUM FAMILY FOUNDATION, INC. was established in 1988 by Alex and Betty Schoenbaum, and annually grants to numerous charitable organizations, including the following in Charleston, West Virginia: Boy Scouts of America, Charleston Civic Center, Charleston Light Opera Guild, Inc., Children's Home Society of West Virginia, Community Council of Kanawha Valley, Covenant House, Daymark Inc., Junior Achievement of Kanawha Valley, Kanawha Hospice Care, Kanawha Valley Fellowship Home, Keep a Child in School, Manna Meal, Mountaineer Food Bank, Mountaineer Habitat for Humanity, Nature Conservancy of West Virginia, United Way of Kanawha Valley, Women's Health Center of West Virginia, and YWCA of Charleston.

Some of the major philanthopies of Betty Schoenbaum since Mr. Schoenbaum's passing on December 6, 1996

INCLUDE:

- ➢ Establishment of a human services center in Charleston, West Virginia, to house nonprofit social services agencies, named the Schoenbaum Family Enrichment Center in memory of Alex Schoenbaum.

- ➢ Establishment of 6 charitable lead annuity trusts in 1998 whereby 22 different charities located in Sarasota,

- ➢ Florida, Charleston, West Virginia and Columbus, Ohio, benefited annually until 2012 with an endowment. Some of the beneficiaries in Sarasota are All Faiths Food Bank, The Glasser/Schoenbaum Human Services Center, Jewish Family & Children's Service of Sarasota-Manatee, Inc., The Pines of Sarasota, Sarasota Ballet of Florida, Inc. (for young people), Sarasota-Manatee Jewish Federation (for Tel Mond Library Fund), Family Law Connection and Women's Resource Center of Sarasota County, Inc. Some of the benefiting charities in Charleston, West Virginia, are Congregation B'nai Jacob (for Computer Education Center), Manna Meal, Inc. and West Virginia Symphony. In Columbus, Ohio, The Ohio State University (for benefit of Critical Difference for Women) is a beneficiary.

- Paid for renovation and improvement of City of Charleston Tennis Courts.

- Paid for a 2 ½ story Library at the University of Charleston in Charleston, West Virginia.

- Major contribution to the new undergraduate College of Business building at The Ohio State University, which is named Schoenbaum Hall.

- Endowed scholarships at West Virginia University and The Ohio State University.

- Endowed scholarships at Women's Resource Center of Sarasota County, Inc., Sarasota, Florida.

- Establishment of an endowed scholarship fund for the College of Education at The Ohio State University, Columbus, Ohio.

- Scholarships awarded annually to students of Johnson & Wales University's Culinary Arts and Keystone College's Culinary Arts from The Schoenbaum Scholarship Foundation which was founded and funded by Alex Schoenbaum.

- Funding for production of the video anthology SPORTS AND OUR COMMUNITY by Community

- Video Archives.
- Funding to Hadassah for Wolfson Children's Pavilion at Kiryat Hadassah in Jerusalem.
- Funding to Pinellas County Jewish Day School, Clearwater, Florida, for decking in children's lunch area.
- Funding to Sarasota Opera Association for co-production of opening opera annually.
- Funding to Charleston Light Opera Guild for two summer productions annually.
- Major funding to Florida West Coast Symphony Orchestra for Youth Orchestra Endowment.
- Major funding to Boys & Girls Clubs of Sarasota County, Inc., Sarasota, Florida, for Career Development Specialist Office, Ready Set Go Room, Adventures in Learning Room, Performing Arts
- Room, Arts Crafts Room and the Library, and for a Computer Learning Center in a new building in Sarasota, Florida.
- Erected and paid for a 2,000-seat soccer arena and amphitheater for Coonskin Park in Charleston, West
- Virginia; and paid for Astroturf for soccer field at Coonskin Park.
- Funding for kitchen for use by ballroom at University of Charleston in Charleston, West Virginia.
- Full funding for computer room at Pinellas County Jewish Day School, Clearwater, Florida, and a computer room at B'nai Jacob Synagogue, Charleston, West Virginia; and funding for a computer center at Goldie

Feldman Academy at Temple Beth Sholom, Sarasota, Florida.

- Establishment of a special scholarship fund at Women's American ORT in memory of Alex Schoenbaum.

- Conceived and major funded the Schoenbaum Family Center at Weinland Park, a 40,000 sq. ft. early childhood education research lab for children from birth to 5 years old, partnered with the College of Human Ecology at The Ohio State University in Columbus, Ohio.

- -Full funding for the Alex and Betty Schoenbaum Science, Educational, Cultural & Sports Campus for Ethiopian Jews in Kiryat Yam, Israel, which was dedicated in October 2011, including complete remodeling of Rodman High School, which was built in 1946.

- Fully funded a new Performing Arts Stage on the levee in the City of Charleston, West Virginia.

- Major funding in 2013 for the construction of a 12,000 sq. ft. Babies and Children's Medical Center at

- Glasser/Schoenbaum Human Services Center, a 44,000 sq. ft. complex of 13 buildings housing 17 nonprofit organizations.

ADDITIONAL:

- One of the founders of Alexis de Tocqueville Society in Sarasota, Florida, and a member in Charleston, West Virginia, since inception.

- Contributor to the United Jewish Appeal for 67 years.

- Member of Lion of Judah in Charleston, West Virginia.

- Member of Lion of Judah in Sarasota, Florida, with an Endowed Pin.

- Recipient of Honorary Degree, Doctor of Humanities, in May 1999 at University of Charleston, in Charleston, West Virginia.

- Recipient of Women of Achievement Award in February 2000 from YWCA Charleston, in Charleston, West Virginia.

- Recipient of Honorary Degree, Doctor of Business, in March 2001 at the Ohio State University in Columbus, Ohio.

- Recipient of the Distinguished West Virginian Award presented by Governor Bob Wise on April 26, 2001 at the Glass Breaking Ceremony for the Schoenbaum Family Enrichment Center, Charleston, WV.

- Recipient of Everett D. Reese Medal September 27, 2002, for exceptional lifetime service in private philanthropy for The Ohio State University.

- Recipient of Women of Power Recognition at National Council of Jewish Women luncheon on January 22, 2003, in Sarasota, Florida.

- Recipient of YMCA Spirit of the Valley Award in August 2004 from YMCA Charleston in Charleston, West Virginia.

- Recipient of Women of Community Impact honor from United Way of Sarasota County in February 2005.

- Inducted into Hall of Fame at West Virginia University College of Human Resources and Education on March 30, 2006.

- Recipient of Human Relations Award from American Jewish Committee on January 25, 2007.

- Recipient of '2007 Irene Bandy-Hedden Early Learning and School Readiness Leadership Award' in the conceptual category from Ohio Department of Education for vision, leadership and financial contribution to children, families and community through the establishment of the Early Childhood Development Center at Weinland Park in Columbus, Ohio.

- Recipient of medal representing membership in the 1880 Society (major donors of World ORT), in September 2008.

- Recipient of Charleston Gazette-Mail's 2008 West Virginian of the Year in December 2008.

- Recipient of Legacy of Leadership Award from American Jewish Committee in March 2009.

- Recipient of "Do the Charleston" Award from Charleston Area Alliance in Charleston, WV, February 9, 2010.

- Recipient of Robert M. Duncan Alumni Citizenship Award in Columbus, Ohio, September 24, 2010.

- Appointment as an Honorary Vice President of World ORT at World ORT Assembly in June 2012.

- Induction into Community Video Archives Hall of Fame, Sarasota, Florida, January 2012.

- Recipient of 2013 Philanthropist of the Year Award from Tampa Bay Biz Journal in October 2013.

- Elected Lifetime Director of the Ohio State University Foundation Board in October 2014.
- Recipient of Lifetime Achievement Award from Jewish National Fund on February 28, 2015.
- Recipient of First Renaissance Woman of the Year Award at Women's Resource Center Luncheon March 9, 2015.
- Recipient of Shining Stars Citizen of the Year Award from SCOSA in Sarasota on March 25, 2015.
- Recipient of Outstanding Alumna of the Year Award at Alpha Epsilon Phi National Convention in Norfolk, Virginia, on June 24, 2017.

Gus Mollasis is a writer, author, filmmaker and film teacher. His Acclaimed *PBS TV Series Diamonds Along The Highway -Florida Stories,* returns for a third season in 2018. He can be seen on the pages of Scene magazine penning his monthly Interview segment –Scenes from An Interview or teaching film around town at venues like the Longboat Key Education Center. An author of two books, one on his beloved Detroit Red Wings – On a Wing and Prayer, the other a biography on one of his heroes, Detroit Lions Hall of Famer Lem Barney. He is busy finishing a biography on Detroit TV and Advertising Icon – Mr. Belvedere- Bud Lezell. Gus is inspired by the philosophy of his writing hero Ernest Hemingway secret to good writing- "All you have to do is write one true sentence."

CPSIA information can be obtained
at www.ICGtesting.com
Printed in the USA
LVHW101130070423
743751LV00004B/116/J